.95

71-2154

SEE PARRIS AND DIE:
BRUTALITY IN THE
U.S. MARINES

SEE PARRIS AND DIE

BRUTALITY IN THE
U.S. MARINES

by

H. Paul Jeffers

and

Dick Levitan

Foreword by Representative Mario A. Biaggi

HAWTHORN BOOKS, INC.
Publishers
NEW YORK

SEE PARRIS AND DIE

Acknowledgments

Considerable effort goes into every book, and not all of it comes from the author. So thanks are in order to those who have contributed so much to this book. We express our appreciation to Mrs. Dolores Concepción for her cooperation in helping us tell the tragedy of her young husband and for her confidence that if she came to us, we would be able to help. We hope we have lived up to her confidence and to that of others who have expressed their wish that our efforts would serve to hasten the day when brutality and inhumanity will not be a part of service in the United States Marines. We want to thank the many Marines and former Marines who talked with us about the Corps. Among these we single out Frank Goerg, executive editor of WINS, New York. Frank's interest and encouragement are much appreciated. His tales of his own service in the Corps were not only helpful but often hilariously entertaining.

For her work at the typewriter, transcribing hours of tape-recorded interviews, and for her insights and intuition in interpreting many of those interviews, we thank Trudy Levitan. Thanks, too, to Catherine Lynch for her help and advice in our library research. For the hours he spent leafing through periodicals and books, we express our gratitude to Kirk Maurer. For their help in converting raw research material into a manuscript, we thank Hedy Bergida and John Hawkins.

We feel we should add a word about one particular platoon of Marine recruits that we encountered at Parris

Island. They were going through some rigorous exercises as we approached them, but they finished before we reached their training area. The officer who was escorting us ordered their DI to have the recruits go through the exercises again so we could tape them. The last thing in the world that we wanted was to add to the burdens of Marine recruits, so to them we offer our thanks and our apologies.

—H. P. J. and D. L.
New York City

Contents

Foreword

The grand ballroom of Los Angeles' Century Plaza hotel glittered. Looking down from the imposing dais was the President of the United States, host to a spectacular state dinner honoring the Apollo 11 astronauts. Into the midst of this largest and most prestigious gathering of American and foreign celebrities ever invited to dine with the President of the United States marched a line of musicians, sturdy and handsome, dressed in brilliant red tunics, their brass and their silvered drums glinting beneath the television lights. This was the United States Marine Band, and when they blared into the most famous of all American Service songs, "The Marines' Hymn," they brought the President of the United States and his guests to their feet for prolonged cheers and applause.

So it was and so it had always been, as the words of the *Hymn* proclaimed, "Admiration of the Nation . . . the finest ever seen . . . ."

But in the past several months, I have seen another side of the United States Marine Corps, a side that has caused me the deepest anguish and anxiety. I have seen cases of brutality and racism in our troubled Corps, and I have felt that these cases—not isolated ones—have been demeaning to the men involved and to the Corps in which they serve.

I believe this is a story that must be told fully for the good of the Corps and the nation. I say this because the problem must not linger, it must not fester until the condition has become so troublesome that the glory, the tradition, the effectiveness, and the greatness of the Corps are in peril. Too many Marines have spilled their blood and given their lives to preserve all of that. We, all of us Americans who care about our nation, owe them nothing less than total involvement to keep the Corps on the pedestal where it belongs.

The authors of this book, H. Paul Jeffers and Dick Levitan, are veteran newsmen who early became aware of the troubles within our Marine Corps, as well as our other armed forces, and who, with me, felt that the full story needed to be told but had not been. If these were writers whose goal was to defame or despoil another great institution of our country—which is, sadly, the fashion today— I would not have entertained their project. But they are as concerned as I and others of my colleagues in the Congress about conditions in all our armed services, although this book deals primarily with the Marines.

In a sense, the history of the United States is a history of the Marines. In fact, the Marines can claim a longer history than the Republic established under our Constitution. The Corps was founded in 1775. Our Constitution was formulated in 1789. The Marines have fought in every American war from the Revolution, when its entire force consisted of two battalions, to Korea, where 75 per cent of its officers and men saw combat, to Vietnam, where its gallant men have fought along the demilitarized zone, in coastal rice paddies, and in the rugged central highlands where the end of the Ho Chi Minh trail pokes its narrow funnel into South Vietnam.

In a war, say the Marines, the only way to survive is to be tough or lucky. "You can't teach luck, so we make Marines tough." That process of turning young civilians into tough, battle-ready Marines occurs over a long period of time, but the basic work is done in boot camp.

Every year, nearly fifty thousand young men travel down

a long palmetto-lined road flanked by a seemingly endless and dismal swamp in the marshy coastal region around Parris Island, South Carolina. At the end of the road lies the United States Marine Recruit Training Depot, which has turned out tough, hard, disciplined men whose purpose was to be the first to fight this country's battles. Most men who go to Parris Island proudly shoulder the burden and the glory of the Marine legend. Most "make it" at Parris Island. Some don't.

But before the Corps lets a man go, it tries hard to keep the man from washing out, to salvage him, to bring him to the level that the Marines expect. It is a stern and demanding process, and no one is arguing about the rightness of being tough to get a man into shape.

Unfortunately, stern discipline has sometimes crossed the line to become brutality. A Jewish recruit whose mind was so tormented he thought he was in a concentration camp; a youth who was savagely beaten after being made to swallow canteens full of water and died four days later of his injuries; countless recruits slugged, kicked, slapped, and shoved far beyond the requirements of discipline; prisoners in jail whose treatment can only be called primitive; and a rampant disregard for the basic civil rights that belong to all Americans whether civilian or soldier—these are the sad tales of our troubled Corps today.

Since 1965, courts-martial have been ordered for threescore Parris Island Drill Instructors, and more than half have been convicted.

The brutality is often rooted in sadism, racism, and religious prejudice.

Unfortunately, until now, the scope and depth of the brutality, racism, and injustice in the Marine Corps have not been fully reported to the American people.

I have investigated reports of brutality and racism on

some military installations. Once my investigations began, I found that I was receiving an outpouring of responses from Americans who were concerned about what was happening in the Corps.

A typical letter came from a woman who had a real concern for the safety and well-being of her son:

> Dear Mr. Biaggi:
> God bless you always for showing an interest in the brutalities at Parris Island. My seventeen-year-old son was there in 1967. He begged me to pray for him in his letters. He said that if anyone would report the Drill Instructors for their cruelties everyone would be punished and even more so. The Drill Instructors should learn that training and brutality are two different subjects. It's still going on in Okinawa, where my son is now. Please forgive me for not giving my address. I don't want my son punished or have the same thing happen as happened to José L. Concepción.
> Thank you for your good work.

José Concepción, as this book relates, died under mysterious and still unsatisfactorily explained circumstances at Parris Island in July, 1969.

My investigations uncovered other cases of brutality and death in the Marines, but it also revealed another shocking condition which also needs correcting. Incredibly, these people apparently had had no one to whom to turn. Again and again they reported that they had sought redress from the Marines or from the Congressional committee whose job it is to oversee the conduct of our armed services, but to no avail.

My own investigation of conditions at military installations met stiff resistance from the House Committee on Armed Services, whose chairman is L. Mendel Rivers of South Carolina.

As I stated in a speech on the floor of the House, "It is sad but accurate to say at this time that American boys are not only dying on foreign soil, but their lives are also obviously being jeopardized needlessly right within the confines of some of our own military installations. That, in my opinion, is sufficient reason alone for objective procedure."

My suggestion in the form of a resolution to set up a new watchdog committee on the military with special concerns for the rights of our servicemen met stern opposition from Mr. Rivers' committee, which, unfortunately, must be considered very much a part of the Pentagon Establishment. The House Committee on Armed Services virtually controls the placing of military contracts, the building of military installations, and other military spending. Congressmen who invoke the displeasure of the committee and its chairman run a serious risk of damaging their states and Congressional districts because of the real possibility of discrimination against those areas when military decisions on sites and spending are being made by the committee. All of this, it seems to me, at the expense of the individual GI, who finds there is no place to turn for help.

To aid these men, I proposed an independent select committee of the House to conduct inquiries into all aspects of crime and disorder on military installations. Such a committee would determine root causes, compile findings, and recommend fair and equitable procedures for correcting the problems that now exist.

The Armed Services Committee bridled at the thought, letting it be known that these were the province of its members and chairman.

Investigation of conditions at military installations meets further difficulties from the military itself. A Congressman arriving at a base gets the red-carpet treatment. The place has been cleaned up, sanitized, and made neat. Courtesy and cool drinks greet the Congressmen at the main gate, and underlying the flattering VIP treatment is a concerted effort to sweep untidy matters under the rug. My own investigations quickly took the form of unannounced visits, further irritating the military Establishment.

The authors of this book met the same problems, although they did not have the added burden of possibly facing subtle sanctions from an all-powerful House committee for their efforts.

The authors found, as did I, that the way to probe alleged problems at military installations is not by sitting down and breaking bread with the brass.

This book does not break bread with the military. Nor does it intend to be hostile, as is the present vogue. Its purpose is to tell the facts as they are, and they are not pretty.

Brutality and death on the battlefield are the unavoidable results of war and are intricately interwoven into the legend of the Marines. In war, Marines give no quarter and expect none.

But brutality and death on the training ground and in the barracks can only tarnish the nation's pride in its Marines.

This is a report on what two reporters' investigations into the Marine Corps have revealed. It isn't pleasant, but it is true. It is written not to malign the Marines but in the hope and belief that it will help to restore and maintain the honor, prestige, and glory of the United States Marine Corps.

MARIO A. BIAGGI
Member of Congress
Washington, D.C.

CHAPTER ONE

SEE PARRIS AND DIE

*His canteen wasn't full at all. So he
punched him once, and he fell against
his rack, and then he hit him again and
again until he fell to the ground on his
knees after he finished hitting him.*

A letter from a Marine

The sun scorched the rifle range all day long. It was Friday, June 28, 1968, and it was the final day on the range, the
last evening of the two weeks that Platoon 262 would be
spending in the Weapons Battalion. All day long the range
barked with the report of weapons. The air clicked with
the sounds that bullets make hitting taut paper targets. The
voice of the range officer boomed out of loudspeakers, and
the now-familiar voices of Drill Instructors rasped the
stifling air. Yet Private Tommy Bartolomeo felt good,
damned good. He'd qualified, shooting pretty well for a kid
who'd never used a rifle before the Marines.

Standing back from the firing line, proud of his score,
Private Bartolomeo was beginning to believe that he'd be
a Marine after all. A small boy, 5 feet 7½ inches tall
and weighing 140 pounds, he had black hair, brown eyes,

1

and a ready smile, even when the going was rough in Platoon 262.

The going had been rough from the beginning of boot camp, as Tommy and the others had expected, but none of them expected to find a man quite like Staff Sergeant George J. Janatsch, Jr., one of the platoon's two Assistant Drill Instructors.

"Man, he's an animal," said one of the recruits early in the training cycle. It was a nickname applied to most DI's by most recruits. DI's refer to recruits as animals also, and this term has led, naturally, to a nickname for the barracks, which are known as "barns" among recruits. But the men of Platoon 262 felt their nickname for Sergeant Janatsch was truly apt. He was a man of moods and had a bad temper, as nearly every recruit in the platoon could swear.

"Well, we've all qualified," said Tommy's buddy, "so I guess nobody's going to get beaten."

"I guess not," Tommy said, whispering.

"Be glad to get off this range and outta this Weapons Battalion," Tommy's friend said, also whispering.

"You privates knock it off," boomed the familiar voice of Sergeant Janatsch.

The last rounds barked in the afternoon heat, and presently Platoon 262 fell in for the march back to the barracks for packing of gear and the return to "main-side" in the morning. Soon there would be evening chow. It would be more welcome than ever, because the day on the qualification range had been long, hot, and hard.

There was no relief from the heat in the squad bay as the platoon fell out to wash up for chow, but there was little time anyway before the DI was yelling, calling them back into formation for the march to the mess hall. It seemed like hours before the line of young men moved stiffly through the mess hall door and into another line to pass by the steam tables. Holding their gleaming metal trays flat against their chests until they reached the first of the serving stations, then passing quickly through the line, Tommy and his friend took seats with other buddies from the platoon and began eating. Someone made a whispered comment about one of the DI's from another platoon and everyone stifled laughter, but Tommy hadn't heard the comment and didn't know what the joke was. Later he would ask his buddy and enjoy the laugh then, he decided.

Across the room, several DI's stood grim-faced and straight, watching, counting the allotted twenty minutes for chow. Their presence threw a blanket of silence over the mess hall.

Tommy ate quickly, wanting to get out into the air again, no matter how hot it was.

The march back to the barracks was helped by a breeze that came up from the ocean.

Standing at attention and waiting to be dismissed so they could go inside and begin packing gear, the men of Platoon 262 kept their eyes straight ahead, seeing Sergeant Janatsch pacing in front of the formation. Obviously, he was in a mood. He stopped, at last, turned, and started talking about some shitheads making fun of another DI in the mess hall. Shithead stuff like that was very embarrassing. Shithead stuff like that would have to stop. Shitheads would have to learn a lesson.

The orders were quite clear: everybody was to go inside the barracks, into the head, and fill their canteens with water.

Platoon 262 fell out and went inside, dutifully filling their canteens, each holding about a quart of water.

Next, the order was to drink the water. No one was to take the canteen from his lips until the canteen was empty.

The men drank.

Fill them again, came the order.

Drink the water down, all of it, no stopping!

Someone threw up. Then another. And another.

Fill the canteens again!

Drink again!

Vomit splashed over the floor of the squad bay.

Fill them again!

Slipping in their own vomit, lurching and staggering into the head, Platoon 262 filled their canteens again.

"I can't drink anymore," Tommy Bartolomeo gasped. "I'm sick, man. I can't."

His buddy told him he'd better fill it.

"I can't. I can't," Tommy muttered, staggering away from the sink, his canteen nearly empty.

Inside the squad bay, the platoon stood by the bunks, canteens in hand, waiting. Sergeant Janatsch walked slowly along the ranks, checking each canteen.

Later, in a letter to Tommy's parents, his buddy explained what happened:

> He came around to each man and checked each canteen to see if the man had filled it up. I had told Tommy to fill his canteen but didn't think about what was going to happen. I wish I would of made him fill it. So he went down the line and checked each person's canteen when he came to Tommy. His canteen wasn't full at all. So he punched him once, and he fell against his rack, and then he hit him again and again until he fell to the ground on his knees after he finished hitting him. That night Tommy had pains all over, he said.

Next day, the platoon returned "main-side"—back to their regular platoon barracks at the Recruit Training Regiment in the heart of Parris Island.

Back at the platoon "barn" that Saturday, Tommy Bartolomeo was in agony. That night he vomited blood. The next day he went to the sick bay and from there to the U.S. Navy Hospital at nearby Beaufort, where he was examined by Commander Peter A. Flynn, of the Navy medical corps.

Diagnosing gastric bleeding, the doctor determined that surgery would be required. It was performed on July 2 by Navy Commander Bruce K. Defiebre, Jr. Both doctors indicated that they found no bruises on the boy's stomach or abdomen as would be expected "if the patient had received a severe blow to the abdomen." Dr. Defiebre also stated that he found "no evidence of injury" but instead found a "fresh gastric ulcer" that was "bleeding slowly."

The doctor noted that the boy had "a bleeding acute gastric ulcer and hemorrhagic gastritis"—conditions, he noted, that are "often associated with psychological stress or prolonged physical stress such as seen in severe chronic illness or in a severely burned patient." The doctor concluded in a statement that "there was no evidence to substantiate a causal relationship between the alleged maltreatment of Pvt. Bartolomeo and his development of gastric bleeding."

Surgery was performed on Tommy Bartolomeo, but on July 21 he died, the cause of death listed as peritonitis. This condition arose, according to the autopsy performed on him, because his postoperative course was complicated with recurrent bleeding, wound infection, failure of wound healing, ultimately requiring four more operative procedures and transfussions of more than a hundred units of whole blood. His condition had gradually deteriorated.

The autopsy concluded, "Too much has happened to this boy to be able to interpret clearly the most initial occurrences. Even the disease process for which his initial surgery was performed is obscured by the subsequent changes."

The autopsy could show the ultimate cause of Tommy Bartolomeo's death but was unable to determine the original cause of his need for surgery. There were conflicting reasons:

—Two Navy doctors stated that he suffered from a fresh bleeding ulcer.

—His Marine buddies testified to a beating by Sergeant Janatsch.

On the basis of the doctors' report, no action was taken against Janatsch by the Marine Corps, but the parents of Tommy Bartolomeo were not satisfied with the official explanations of their son's death. The letter received from Tommy's buddy detailing the incident with the canteens had convinced them that their son died as a result of injuries during that beating. In the letter, Tommy's buddy stated that Tommy had many friends in Platoon 262 who would also testify to the accuracy of his buddy's description of the canteen incident, despite the fact that "some of them are worried about getting hurt."

Fear of reprisal for what they may tell about cases of maltreatment or brutality often keeps young Marines from speaking out. Time and time again in the course of interviews for this book, the authors found witnesses reluctant to talk because of fear of reprisal. One Marine reservist was fearful of what he might be subjected to during his annual two weeks of training if he cooperated in the preparation of this book. One man in a brig said with an ironic smile, "You will leave here, sir, but I have to stay." We came across numerous instances in which Marines told us that they had been warned that Drill Instructors are a tightly knit group who will stick together. The thrust of this threat is that no matter where a man goes, he will always find another Marine who has been a Drill Instructor and who will feel obligated to settle the score for a DI who was punished because of someone's testimony. The warning, in effect, to recruits who witness brutality or maltreatment is, "I have buddies in other camps who will deal with you if you tell what happened. If I lose any stripes, I'll get even with you."

Even so, such threats had no effect on Tommy's buddy, who wrote, "I figure nothing can hurt me now, because in about two months I'll be in Vietnam, so who cares? I really treasure my life and no one is going to take it away from me."

The Bartolomeo family contacted Representative John W. Wydler of New York and asked his aid in resolving the matter of their son's death and the beating he received prior to it from Sergeant Janatsch. "We demand that Sgt. Janatsch be brought up and face court-martial and be punished for his crimes," they wrote.

In November, 1968, nearly three months after Tommy Bartolomeo died, Sergeant Janatsch was court-martialed on charges of maltreatment and assault, to which he pleaded guilty. He was not charged with murder because of the testimony of the two doctors and the autopsy report, even though it had been unable to determine what caused the boy's massive internal damage because "too much" had been done to him. Janatsch was sentenced to two years in prison, reduction to private, forfeiture of pay, and a bad conduct discharge.

Public attention, such as it was, faded.

No attention was paid to the next steps in the Janatsch case—automatic reviews of his penalties by higher authorities. These higher authorities reduced the prison sentence to six months, removed the penalty of forfeiture of pay, and rescinded the bad conduct discharge. The authorities based their findings on two factors: first, the two-year term was illegally imposed, a fact that should have been known at the time of the original sentencing; second, Janatsch had an "exemplary" combat record. The review procedure permitted Janatsch to stay in the Marines.

When the Bartolomeo family learned this, they were horrified. They wrote again to Representative Wydler, asking him to use his influence to see that Janatsch would not be permitted to reenlist in the Marines:

Knowing Pvt. Janatsch will not have any authority over any recruits for the remainder of his enlistment is a comfort to us. But knowing he can reenlist and may work his way up to authority again makes us sick.

This man is a sadist and should've been discharged.

You see, Mr. Wydler, we received a copy of the testimony the recruits of Platoon 262 gave at the hearing and the trial. The way the boys were mistreated and beaten, you would never believe this man could only receive the sentence he did.

We also received a copy of the autopsy report. We had a pathologist read it for us. This man was shocked at what he read. So you see, knowing Janatsch is going about his merry way doesn't comfort us in any way.

It seems the only way to survive today is to go to college and to protest, to burn your country's flag, or even to burn your draft card. You're protected by the law. If our son were of this caliber he might've been alive today. Instead, he chose to protect his country and his freedom by going into the service when his country called.

We taught our children to respect God, country, and authority. We taught them that this was the greatest country to live in. Instead, he received a vicious beating from one of his own countrymen. This was his reward. It shakes one's loyalty toward one's own country.

Mr. Wydler, how do you explain to Tommy's sister? How do you explain that all men aren't like that? Yet everyone we talk to knows someone who has gone through boot training at Parris Island and received a vicious beating at one time or another. The list is endless. Can we still tell her that this is still the greatest country to live in, when we're not so sure ourselves?

We realize there will always be men like Janatsch, but when the military condones such actions!

It's a sad day for all of us.

Please, God, help us to forgive.

To the Bartolomeo family, Wydler wrote, "Let me assure you that I have every intention of contacting the Commandant of the Marine Corps in January, 1970, to urge that George Janatsch not be permitted to reenlist."

Janatsch served his six months term and then spent the

rest of his time in the Marines tending sailboats at the Parris Island yacht basin. He did not reenlist, but his removal from the Corps does not end maltreatment and brutality. It was, sadly, only one episode in a long history of similar cases.

Waldo Lyon, now a clinical psychologist and mental health coordinator, who served seventeen years as a Navy and Marine psychologist, eight of those years at Parris Island, said in two papers on Marine brutality delivered to the American Orthopsychiatric Association convention in New York on March 31, 1969, that brutality and other maltreatment are so ingrained in the Marines that the Corps could serve as a laboratory for the study of institutionalized violence. Not since 1956, following a notorious incident at Parris Island, had the American people heard such an indictment of the Marines.

Before April 8, 1956, few Americans, unless they were Marines, had heard of Parris Island, South Carolina, but on that date a Marine Drill Instructor marched a platoon of seventy-five trainees on a disciplinary night march into a swamp. Six of the men drowned. The march was ordered by Staff Sergeant Matthew C. McKeon, who was taken into custody and charged with manslaughter, oppression of recruits, and violations of regulations on the use of alcohol. In the trial that followed, McKeon was acquitted of the first two charges but found guilty of negligent homicide and drinking in recruit barracks. He was sentenced to a bad conduct discharge, nine months hard labor, reduction to private, and a $270 fine. These penalties were later reduced by higher authorities and McKeon was discharged from the Corps for medical reasons, three years later.

The McKeon death march and the resulting public furor led to changes in Marine training techniques under new training regulations laid down in April, 1959. Touching the person or clothing of a recruit, either directly or by use of a material object, was banned except when "correcting the recruit's position, correcting his movements, fitting or correcting the arrangement of his clothing or equipment, conducting a lawful examination or inspection of his person." Gentleness was to be the standard in touching a recruit under these conditions.

The new guidelines also banned sundry other traditional hazing activities, such as making recruits run unnecessarily up and down ladders, making them eat or drink more than their normal requirements, causing recruits to participate in assaults on each other, making them stand or stoop in unnatural positions, and making them run into walls. DI's were also banned from "borrowing" money from recruits, a practice that in most situations amounted to extortion under threat.

The commander of Parris Island, Major General Robert Burnstone Luckey, denied that the Corps had been "stampeded" into these changes as a result of public anger after the McKeon affair. But time thereafter at PI has been measured in terms of BM and AM—Before McKeon and After McKeon.

The new Marine Corps regulations on treatment of recruits calmed fears among Americans as the training of Marines settled down once more into routine. It was peacetime, and the recruit training program was geared to a leisurely eleven weeks. But as the United States commitment to Vietnam grew and American ground forces were sent to fight, the demand for battle-ready Marines grew.

In January, 1962, the Commandant of the Corps, General David M. Shoup, watched a platoon of Marines attending a lecture on guerrilla warfare. He said the Marines "looked about as enthusiastic as weight-watching women waiting at a skim-milk dispensary." Shoup thought that his Marines ought to "get out into the rain, snow, cold, and darkness" and "get used to field mice, screech owls, coyotes, and katydids."

By 1965 the Marines whom Shoup had watched with such dismay and disdain were committed to the defense of the Ist Corps area of South Vietnam, where the enemies were not field mice and katydids but excellent, battle-hardened North Vietnamese regulars. Marine Corps training back in the States had to be streamlined to meet the requirements of the war. Pressure was on to turn out Marines, to keep "the pipeline" open and flowing freely with men. The training cycle was reduced to eight weeks, and new pressure was put on Drill Instructors to get their men shaped up and shipped out.

The incidence of recruit maltreatment began a steady upward climb. In a twenty-seven-month period between 1964 and 1966, 120 Drill Instructors were relieved of duty at Parris Island, 73 of them for recruit maltreatment or abuse. About one in nine DI's was relieved.

Colonel James G. Juett, commanding officer of the PI Recruit Training Regiment, defended the new toughness. "The discipline, the physical fitness, the shooting skills that the Drill Instructors teach the recruits may save their lives in combat," he said. He said the training program had not suffered much by being reduced to eight weeks. "We may have lost a little close-order drill, but these Marines are not going to do much close-order drilling in Vietnam."

Some of the men participating in the new, toughened eight-week training period would never get to Vietnam, however.

Between January, 1968, and September, 1969, seventeen Marine recruits died at Parris Island. Of these, according to the Marines, three were drownings, three were suicides, one was listed as accidental choking, and the other ten were listed as natural deaths from pneumonia, heart failure, brain abscess, pulmonary embolism, kidney failure, cardio-respiratory failures, and cardiac arrests. These statistics when recounted by Marine officials sound reasonable, considering the fact that thousands of recruits passed through Parris Island in this period. These deaths would not seem to be out of line with the incidence of death in any other group, but looking deeper into the statistics, one finds that they include some recruits whose apparent natural deaths were associated with systematic exposure to violence and maltreatment.

Maltreatment by Drill Instructors, however, is under-reported and difficult to corroborate, as Mr. Lyon stated in his paper to the American Orthopsychiatric Association. If brutality is reported, in most cases the accused is ac-quitted, or, if found guilty, has his punishment reduced by higher authority on technicalities.

For example, in October, 1958, two years after the Mc-Keon death march three DI's were accused of maltreating recruits and of having taken ten dollars from every one of the sixty-nine recruits in their platoon. The men were cleared of the charges. *The New York Times* noted, "The verdict was boisterously acclaimed by other Drill Instructors at this training base."

In November, 1965, Staff Sergeant Clyde E. Cornelison and two other Drill Instructors were court-martialed on charges of abusing recruits. In the trial eight recruits testified to maltreatment by Cornelison and the others. Cornelison denied the accusations but admitted to "touching" one of the men, Private Douglas W. Boone, of Great Falls, South Carolina "He was the 'fat body' in our barracks. I was feeling his body to see how fat he was and how hard he was breathing," Cornelison testified. Private Boone testified differently, saying, "He took us inside the squad bay and started hitting me in the stomach." Another recruit, Ernest V. Poag, Jr., also of Great Falls, said he was struck on the head by the DI. Cornelison said he "tapped" the re-cruit on the head to remind him not to go out in public without a hat.

On November 19 Cornelison was cleared of all charges.

Another DI, Sergeant Ronald A. Stewart, was accused in this same case of beating seven recruits, the same ones who had testified against Cornelison. In the Stewart proceedings, Private Ralph J. Granger, Jr., testified that he had his first clash with Sergeant Stewart during his second week of training. "He was Sergeant of the Guard," Granger testified. "I was a sentry. And I didn't know what I was supposed to know—who was Officer of the Day, some of the General Orders. He hit me with a rope which had some knots in it." Granger said he was relieved of guard duty and ordered to the guard house. "Then he began to hit me," he testified. "He knocked me down to my knees three times." Sergeant Stewart was found not guilty by the board of officers.

At the time of these trials, the commander at Parris Island, Major General James M. Masters, revealed that charges of maltreatment had been brought against fifty-six DI's between January 1 and October 31, 1965. "This is a little less than 10 per cent of our Drill Instructors," he boasted. "Of these 56, 18 were removed from the field, busted and fined. The other 38 were restored to full duty."

It was apparently quite all right, quite acceptable, to have slightly less than 10 per cent of his complement of DI's charged with maltreatment, and one third of them found guilty and punished. When a commanding general finds it acceptable that eighteen of his DI's were guilty of recruit maltreatment in a period of ten months, one tends to believe the suggestion that the Marine Corps could serve as a laboratory for the study of institutionalized violence.

That Marine training is tough and should be is never the question. No one argues that a man needs to be toughened and disciplined if he is to fight the kind of intense, demanding battles that we require of our Marines. The

question is whether physical brutality and sadism must be
a part of that training. Parris Island's only defense against
charges of brutality is that the training base is not alone,
that a vein of brutality runs through the whole Corps.
True. On April 15, 1966, a DI at San Diego, California,
was accused of beating Private Robert F. Pierce and seriously injuring the recruit by punching him in the kidneys.
Pierce was hospitalized with a kidney ailment and was still
suffering from the ailment when Sergeant Russell P. Arm-
strong, the DI, was tried and acquitted of the charges.

Acquittals are far more numerous than convictions in
cases of alleged maltreatment, and frequently those who
are convicted find their sentences are considerably light-
ened, if not wiped out completely, by the reviews of their
cases by higher authorities. By and large, these men remain in the Corps.

Some of the most severe cases of maltreatment occur in
the Special Training Branch established to handle "problem" cases, the so-called Motivation Platoon.

"The Motivation Platoon is a Marine Corps form of
chain gang," wrote one Marine serving in Vietnam. He had
spent time in "Motivation" at Parris Island and tells of
physical abuse and even death, reporting about one recruit
who allegedly choked to death while running because he
knew that if he fell out he would have been beaten. "I was
sent to Motivation," the Vietnam veteran wrote, "where I
was hit and kicked and denied food."

Another veteran, now out of the Marines with a 60
per cent disability after having suffered a broken neck at
Parris Island, says, "I have seen and been myself assaulted
by a Drill Instructor. I saw a recruit choked until he
passed out. The platoon I was in was put through some
'exercises' that would be considered cruel even by Marine
Corps standards."

Psychologist Waldo Lyon states that the unit for maladjusted recruits at Parris Island meted out more severe pun-

ishments than the brig. One Marine, in a letter to a Congressman, recounted horrifying tales of maltreatment at the Parris Island Motivation Platoon, including the forcing of recruits to beat another recruit with sticks, the kicking and beating of men who fell out during the long, grueling runs to visit Marine monuments, and one instance in which a recruit was allegedly forced to drink his own urine. There may have been exaggerations in some of the tales told by this Marine (who was also on duty overseas at the time he wrote), but there have been enough documented cases of brutalities to add credence to his allegations.

A mother who would not give her name out of fear of reprisal against her son wrote about her boy, who had wanted to be a Marine since he was twelve years old:

> Within two weeks he was kicked in the stomach, choked, beat over the head with the butt of a gun and other forms of brutality too numerous to mention—by his Drill Instructor. My husband and I witnessed his scars on graduation day at Parris Island. He was beaten in both mind and body so badly that we couldn't realize this was our boy. . . . I am sorry that I cannot sign this letter, but I fear for the welfare of my son, who is still in the Marines. Each boy has been warned that if they complained they would "get" them and they would wish that they had not.

The stories do not all come from mothers of Marines. A young Marine serving in Vietnam wrote that the conditions which exist at Parris Island "are a disgrace to young men here in Vietnam." An ex-Marine who was at Parris Island and who served in the Corps until he was honorably discharged states: "Illegal brutality was the rule there, rather than the exception."

Private Steve Melson was to learn that lesson and pay for it with his life.

CHAPTER TWO

PRIVATE STEVE MELSON

You could tell just by looking at him, he was out of it—sluggish, couldn't do any PT. He was sick.

Private Charles D. Calcamp

Money drew Steve Melson to the Marines. He thought he could help his mother and brother by going into the service and sending home his pay. That's the kind of kid eighteen-year-old Steve Melson was.

On September 2, 1969, Steve Melson joined the Marines.

On September 21, Steve Melson died at the Medical University of South Carolina hospital; his death was listed as due to acute kidney failure, uremic encephalopathy, and pneumonia. Apparently Steve had suffered from a kidney ailment before entering the Corps but made no indication of this ailment on his enlistment papers. There is no way of knowing whether he omitted mention of the problem on his own volition or if a Marine recruiter, in need of another man to fill out an enlistment quota, suggested the health

16

problem be overlooked, a practice not uncommon among Marine recruiters under pressure to sign up men.

Before Steve Melson died, he told his mother that he had been beaten by his Drill Instructor. Although doctors said that Steve's death was unrelated to any alleged beatings, Mrs. Melson was not satisfied and demanded explanations from the Marines. Officials at Parris Island denied that the recruit had been beaten.

Then came a letter to Mrs. Melson from a friend of her son's.

"I saw him pushed, kicked, verbally abused by Drill Instructors and other recruits," the friend wrote.

Faced with this allegation, the Marines at Parris Island admitted through information officer Captain M. R. Arnold that "it appears he had suffered some physical abuse prior to going into the hospital."

The abuse, said the Marines, was at the hands of other recruits. "The investigation has revealed evidence which indicates that recruit members of Melson's unit may have struck him in the face and pushed him against the wall on separate occasions because they felt Private Melson was not carrying out his share of the responsibilities of his unit," said Captain Arnold.

He then announced that two Drill Instructors had been suspended from duties during the investigation, although, he said, there was no evidence that Melson had been maltreated by Drill Instructors.

Clearly, there was more to the Melson case than the Marine Corps was willing to admit. Only when presented with accusations disputing their original contention that Melson had not been beaten up by someone did the Parris Island information office admit that the recruit had been maltreated. Forced by facts uncovered by others, the Marines gradually admitted that maltreatment had played a part in the fate of Steve Melson.

One of those who began asking about the Melson case was Representative Biaggi, who was, at this time, also looking into the death of Private José Concepción. What Biaggi discovered, primarily through the testimony of Private Charles D. Calcamp, was a typical case of Marine Corps recruit maltreatment.

On arrival at Parris Island, Melson had been assigned to the Third Recruit Training Battalion. While he was undergoing processing prior to entering regular recruit training, he immediately began having trouble from his chief DI, who finally sent Melson to a unit called a Correctional Custody Platoon (CCP), one of the several special "motivational" units designed to shape up recruits who have special problems. It was while in CCP that Melson met Private Calcamp, himself a member of a Motivation Platoon.

Dom Frasca, Biaggi's aide, interviewed Calcamp:

> FRASCA: Can you tell me precisely what happened down there? What you saw?
>
> CALCAMP: One day the Drill Instructors took us to see some movies on Vietnam and training and so forth, and Private Melson, he was sick. I found out later that he had something wrong with him physically, so he couldn't do what he was told. He just drooped over and the DI wouldn't let him sit down. He kept vomiting, and the DI was standing there harassing him. Then our DI started harassing him, too. Finally, the DI got mad at him because he kept vomiting and kicked him across the classroom until he hit the other side of the room.
>
> FRASCA: Where did he kick him?
>
> CALCAMP: On the side.
>
> FRASCA: That was it?
>
> CALCAMP: He couldn't get up, and the DI kept

harassing him and hit him a few more times. He stayed stooped over all the time. He was hit across the back, sort of a real hard slap, two or three times.

FRASCA: When you saw Melson assaulted, what time of day was it?

CALCAMP: During the day, early afternoon.

FRASCA: A lot of hitting going on there?

CALCAMP: Yes, sir, but they don't let it out. Nobody knows.

FRASCA: Has anybody hit you?

CALCAMP: Yes, sir. Hit by a bayonet. A sergeant hit me in the back.

FRASCA: You have a bad back, don't you?

CALCAMP: Yes, sir. That's why he hit me. If you do something wrong, the DI can beat you to a pulp.

FRASCA: Have you seen DI's beat recruits to a pulp, as you say?

CALCAMP: I've seen DI's beat recruits, yes, sir. There was a DI that we shared a barracks with at the rifle range. He had a big paddle and he worked his recruits over with it.

FRASCA: Was that the only time you saw the Melson boy assaulted, Charlie?

CALCAMP: No. One day in the mess hall the DI hit him because he wouldn't eat lunch. He had to sit at attention and not move, and he wasn't sitting up straight, so the DI hit him—open-handed up the side of the head. This was the same day. The DI's do have recruits beat up on another recruit.

FRASCA: How do they manage that?

CALCAMP: Well, in CCP, their favorite pastime is PT [physical training] all day long, and if one

person fouls up, well then that just increases the
punishment more, and the DI would say, "If you
want to get rid of him, you can have a blanket
party." In that way, they get him out of there.
You see, the DI will suggest this and the other recruits will beat up on this one recruit that can't
keep up. That's what most guys believe happened
to Melson. You could tell just by looking at him,
he was out of it—sluggish, couldn't do any PT.
He was sick.

The story that Calcamp told is accurate, but it took considerable pressure and an outside investigation by a member of Congress to get the Marine Corps to admit what had
happened to Steve Melson.

On November 26, 1969, the Marines announced that two
Drill Instructors had been relieved of their duties. The
Marine Corps admitted that Melson had been maltreated
on several occasions. He had been forced to do bends and
thrusts (a PT exercise), and in so doing, had his feet
kicked out from under him. A DI "shadow boxed" with him
but did not touch him. Three recruits slapped him in the
head and face for "fouling up" their platoon.

For these offenses, two DI's were punished and one was
acquitted. Gunnery Sergeant J. L. Payne was stripped of
DI status and ordered to forfeit three hundred dollars in
pay for violating directives on recruit training. Staff
Sergeant G. G. Thompson was also relieved of his duties.
The three recruits, not identified, were given reprimands
and admonished for improper conduct. The Corps still
maintained that Melson did not die as a result of this maltreatment.

Nonetheless, it is a fact that a young Marine who was
in considerable pain and in need of urgent medical
treatment received, instead, abuse, beatings, and harassment.

To the DI, Melson was just another recalcitrant, another "problem recruit," another "eight ball" to be whipped into shape. No effort was made to determine if the boy was really ill, as he maintained; and to the extent that he was delayed in obtaining medical assistance and subjected to mental and physical anguish on top of his illness, the United States Marines must bear the responsibility for Steve Melson's death. It must bear that responsibility, because it delayed Melson's admission to a hospital until his condition had deteriorated beyond the possibility of help from a kidney machine, a fact conceded by Brigadier General Duane L. Faw, head of the Judge Advocate General Division, USMC.

But the Marine responsibility goes farther back in the history of the Steve Melson case, to the day when he was permitted to enter the Corps with a physical ailment that should have been, and could have been, easily detected by the pre-induction physical examination.

CHAPTER THREE

"I WANT TO JOIN THE MARINES."

Be a man,
Be a Marine.
Recruiting poster

What makes a United States Marine stand out in a crowd? It's more than the uniform. Marines have a way about them. A confidence . . . a coolness . . . a pride all their own. And it shows. In the face . . . in the walk . . . in the spirit of a Marine. The Marine Corps builds men in body, mind, and spirit. Ask a Marine. See your local Marine Corps representative today.

This twenty-second radio announcement is part of a vast array of techniques used by the Marines to recruit. Except in times of war, the Marine Corps is a volunteer outfit, and even in wartime, when a certain number of draftees are assigned to the Marines, the men of the Corps who have volunteered do not really consider the draftees Marines. A Marine is a Marine willingly. He is someone who has walked in the door and said, "I want to join the Marines."

Behind those words lie complex reasons and mental processes that would challenge any psychologist, but if there is a thread of uniformity in the reasons young men have for joining the Marines, it is probably just what the Marines advertise. "The Marine Corps builds men, in body, mind, and spirit."

The recruit is someone who isn't happy with his lot in life. He wants something better—to finish school, to learn a trade, to have respect for himself and from others, to do something, to throw off the label "dropout" or "quitter," to meet a challenge and overcome it. These are goals that our society values and encourages, but a poorly educated, deprived, street-toughened kid from the inner city can't achieve these goals by winning a college scholarship or graduating with honors or tackling the other challenges open to the more privileged. To the kid from a slum, from a ghetto, there are pitifully few means of making something of himself. The uniform of the United States Marines carries with it respect and admiration and the unmistakable statement that "this kid has made it." He's a Marine, and as everyone knows, the Marines are the cream.

A high school dropout is likely to join the Marines. A college dropout isn't. Eighteen-year-old Patrick Backowski from Brooklyn joined the Air Force. He went to all the armed services recruiters *except* the Marines. "Going into the service," he said, "is bad enough. But the Marines, that's twice as bad." He knew that the Marines have courage and guts, as he put it, and that most people have great respect for the Marines, but he didn't feel that he had to prove to anyone that he had the courage that the Marine uniform represents. He had no feeling that the Marine Corps experience could contribute anything to him.

Ramon Rosario felt quite the opposite. About the same age as Backowski—seventeen—Ramon is a light-skinned Puerto Rican. Short, not well built, quiet, and shy, he looks like the delivery boy from the supermarket.

On January 21, 1970, Ramon walked into the Marine Corps recruiting office at 207 West 24th Street, New York City. Following the routine of the recruiting office, Ramon was given an oral interview by a recruiter, a physical examination, and the standard armed forces qualification test, which is a general-knowledge and intelligence quiz. Meantime, his personal records were checked to see if he had a police record. His school records were also checked. Inquiries were made to see if he was a drug user.

Once these preliminaries are out of the way, the would-be enlistee is sent to Fort Hamilton in Brooklyn for an aptitude test. The next day, paper work is done, and the following day the enlistee reports back to Fort Hamilton for actual induction.

Ramon was, however, somewhat a special case because he scored low in the armed forces qualification test, falling into the 16 percentile group, or Category 4 (Cat-4). This low score necessitated an additional interview, which was conducted by Major Charles Van Horn.

"Not everyone comes in to be interviewed by an officer," he explained. "The initial interview is conducted by the recruiters. It's only when the recruiter feels there is some problem about the individual, in other words, these are men who are out of the ordinary for some reason."

Ramon's problem that put him out of the ordinary was his low score on the qualification test. Major Van Horn explained further:

> I will try to determine if the man can basically read, do simple math, times tables, and that he can follow instructions and perform in a manner so that he would be able to survive and get through Parris Island. We try to find out if there are other reasons why the young man scored low. He may have been extremely nervous, or there may be something wrong with the kid's parents, or

he's had an accident. There are myriad reasons why under the circumstances a man would not score well, as well as he would have at some other time. It might be that he speaks Spanish, reads Spanish and yet finishes relatively poor in reading English. Tests are given in English. Had they been given in Spanish, he may have had the intelligence to score extremely well. Are we dealing with intelligence or are we dealing with background and environment?

The interview with the officer will go beyond matters of intelligence and will probe, as deeply as a few minutes permit, into all of those complex motivations that brought the young man in to see the Marine recruiter. Major Van Horn got right to the question of motivation:

MAJOR: Ramon, why do you want to join the Marine Corps?

RAMON: For the training.

MAJOR: For the training? What do you know about the training?

RAMON: Physical training. Riflery, combat training.

MAJOR: Did your recruiter tell you about this, or do you have friends in the Marine Corps?

RAMON: I got friends in the Marine Corps.

MAJOR: How old are you?

RAMON: I'm seventeen, going on eighteen.

MAJOR: What do your parents think of your going in the Marine Corps?

RAMON: They don't think nothing.

MAJOR: They know you might have to go Vietnam? What do you think your chances are of going to Vietnam?

RAMON: Fifty-fifty, maybe.

MAJOR: How do you feel about that?

RAMON: It's all right.

MAJOR: You live at home with your parents?

RAMON: I live with my mother.

MAJOR: Are your parents separated, or is your father dead?

RAMON: No, I don't know my father.

MAJOR: How much school have you had?

RAMON: About second year.

MAJOR: Why did you leave school?

RAMON: I wanted to be with my friends.

MAJOR: What are you going to do if you get down to Parris Island and you don't like it? You're not going to be able to play hookey. I'll show you why you are not going to be able to play hookey.

The major produced a small printed card and handed it to Ramon, asking the boy to read it. The card stated that Parris Island is surrounded by marshes, swamps, and tidal waters as well as quicksand and poisonous snakes. It warns of the dangers of trying to swim away. The card is both a test of a boy's ability to read and a test of his nerves, warning him of Parris Island's terrors.

MAJOR: Can you swim, Ramon?

RAMON: Not that great.

MAJOR: Well, you better not try to play hookey at Parris Island. How's your mathematics? Can you add, subtract, multiply?

RAMON: Yes.

MAJOR: Divide?

RAMON: Not so good.

MAJOR: Know your times tables?

RAMON: Some of them.

[Ramon had great difficulty, needing paper and pencil to figure six times eight.]

MAJOR: Did you like your teachers when you were in school?

RAMON: Yes.

MAJOR: How come you didn't stick around?

RAMON: I used to play around with the girls.

MAJOR: What does your girl friend think of your going in the Marine Corps?

RAMON: Not so good.

MAJOR: Read the newspaper much?

RAMON: Yes.

MAJOR: Who is the Vice-President of the United States?

RAMON: Nixon.

MAJOR: No, he used to be. You know who the new Vice-President is?

RAMON: I ain't read a newspaper lately.

MAJOR: Let me tell you, Ramon, what will happen to you in the Marine Corps. You get on an airplane. You fly down to Charleston, South Carolina. You'll get on a bus that'll pick you up and take you to Parris Island. You'll be with a group of other people just like yourself. Bus'll take you on the base, a beautiful base with trees with Spanish moss and a golf course. Very pretty. You'll drive down a big boulevard. The bus'll pull up in front of the receiving barracks. Man in front of the bus will stand up and say, "All right, the smoking lamp is out. You've got ten seconds to get out of this bus and stand in those marks." You look out of the window and you'll see all these painted footprints on the pavement. Then the screaming starts, and the yelling, and everyone tries to get off that bus first and stand on those marks. After they get through screaming at you, they'll take you inside the barracks. First thing you do is take off all your clothes and

throw them in a bag and send them home to
Mother. You don't need those things anymore.
They give you anything you need and take away
anything you don't need. Then the next thing
we take away that you don't need—your hair.
You go in and they give you the fastest haircut
in the world, and then you'll be just as ugly as
everyone else down there. Then they take you
in for a shower to wash away that hair, sort of
like a baptism, 'cause you're goin' to be a new
man. You're going to put on new clothes. Going
to take you to the doctor, dentist, and psychiatrist
to give you more tests. Corpsman going to give
you needles in the arm, catch you up on all your
shots, then turn you over to the Drill Instructor.
Have you ever heard of a Drill Instructor,
Ramon?

RAMON: Yes.

MAJOR: He's a very bad man. He's a staff sergeant and has two assistants. One of these men
will be with you twenty-four hours a day, seven
days a week for eight weeks. They don't like you.
They think you made a bad mistake about seventeen years ago. They only have eight weeks to
change you, to make you somebody they'd like to
go into combat with. They're going to scream on
you, call you bad names, make you run until you
fall, then run some more. You ready for that?

RAMON: Yes.

MAJOR: Okay. Go out there and see the man who
interviewed you when you first came in here this
morning.

With that, Ramon Rosario had joined the Marines.
"He reads better than most kids like him that I see," ex-

plained Major Van Horn. "He won't have any problems the way things are taught. It'll be gone over enough times so that he won't have any problems with reading. His math? He knows all he has to know."

While the Marines at recruiting may gloss over deficiencies in a man's mental capacities, they are scrupulous about their probing to discover if enlistees use drugs.

"If a man indicates that he's had any experience with drugs, he's rejected," explained Major Van Horn.

If drug use is not detected before enlistment, it is easy to see within the first two weeks of training that a man has been on drugs. Once detected, rehabilitation is attempted; if it fails, the man is discharged from the Corps for ineptitude.

According to Major Van Horn, Ramon Rosario's chances of getting successfully through Parris Island boot camp were 6 to 1 in his favor, despite his score in Category 4 in the mental test.

> I feel that a Cat-4 from this area [New York City], from the inner city, has a much better chance than one from the hills of Kentucky or someplace like that because a man from the inner city lives in a jungle where he has to survive and be quick. He's going into another type of jungle when he goes into boot training. There's going to be a lot of pressure on him all the time. I think Ramon reacts better to it than a man from rural areas would.

Master Sergeant Peter Frano, an eighteen-year Marine veteran, area supervisor for recruiting for Brooklyn, Queens, Nassau, and Suffolk counties, feels that he has the easiest recruiting job around because he believes he has "one of the best products in the country to sell—the U.S. Marine Corps."

He explains, in his view, why young men join up: "They

are looking for a way of life or a challenge to exercise freedom in themselves. They feel that if they go in the Marine Corps as a recruit, they have a challenge."

How do today's recruits compare to recruits of the past?

"The individuals that we have right now are smarter by far than they were fifteen years ago, sixteen years ago, twenty years ago. They are stronger, bigger, quicker to learn. Right now the recruits who walk into the recruiting office are more highly qualified than they were years ago, education-wise, physically and mentally," Sergeant Frano believes.

Lieutenant Colonel William J. Hallisey, Jr., in charge of recruiting for New York and New Jersey, is a man in his forties with graying hair, deep-set eyes, and a way of looking at you squarely when he talks to you. He is soft-spoken and tends to philosophize, something which he feels he has to apologize for. He is fully aware of the hardships that await the young men who pass through his recruiting stations. He feels that Marine recruit training is the last bastion of the hard approach toward discipline in a society that he regrets is now filled with permissiveness. He says he fully understands how this kind of training can be a devastating awakening to young men who have grown up with permissive parents who accepted Dr. Spock as gospel.

"My function, as a recruiter," he says, "is twofold: to be as much a counselor to the young men who come in as a recruiter for military service. The field of military service and planning your future is so involved and there are so many different sources of information that one of the principal occupations of a military recruiter is counseling on how to have the military obligation mesh with the planned future a young man sees for himself."

Hallisey considers military training as much an educational process as high school and college. The uneducated man in military service is lost, he feels.

"A man without education starts behind the eight ball in terms of being able to be trained. We need a man that we can train, that we can teach, and if he has failed in the teaching process during his youth, he's more likely to fail in our teaching process when we get him into our schools. The only reason we take dropouts is because we are required to take them."

What kind of quota system does the metropolitan New York area have on an average? It depends on several factors, not the least of which is the overall national quota for men in all the services. The New York area Marine recruiters commonly must provide 7 per cent of the national quota. If that quota is not met through enlistments, the remainder will be drawn from the Selective Service pool, a resolution of the quota dilemma as repulsive to the Marine Corps as it may be to the men drafted into the Corps.

Admitting that Marine special training in specialized schools and skills is similar, if not identical, to training in other services, Colonel Hallisey summed up from his recruiting experience why certain men, given the choice of all the services, join the Marines:

I feel it is the disciplined life that the Marine Corps espouses and develops, the disciplined approach to life. The period of training a man initially undergoes when he joins the Marines, this eight weeks of training, is a deliberately highly stressed environment with the idea in mind that he knows his whole capabilities, both mental and physical, have been tested. He has passed through the roughest training-type of test that he will ever encounter in any military service. It builds within him a sense of confidence in his own abilities, and in a young man this is the transition that takes place from being a boy to being a man, the confidence in your own ability to do a job. This is possibly the single most important thing that they'll get out of being a Marine.

There is no question that a young man who has gone
through the rigors of Marine training and who has earned
the name Marine feels a towering pride in that achievement. No Marine or former Marine interviewed for this
book ever denied a certain pride in the name, although
many were critical of certain aspects of the Corps and had
their own personal gripes and bitternesses. But Marines to
a man seem enormously proud of having served in the Corps
and clearly reflect a belief that they have met a challenge
to them as men. This attitude, found in all Marine recruiters and Drill Instructors, is, of course, vital to the
spirit of the Corps. It has welded this most remarkable
military organization together, not just for brief periods
of stress or national crisis, but for the nearly two hundred years of the Corps's existence. Pride in being a Marine is a remarkable phenomenon, and that obvious pride
is what appeals to the young men today who turn to the
Marines for their own special challenges.

Times are changing, however, and the Marine Corps,
like all services, faces an increasing pacifism among our
youth, whose open scorn for the military encroaches steadily on the need of the Corps to flesh out its ranks. The fairly
affluent white youths who once joined the Marines as a
matter of personal challenge now seriously question
whether those are the challenges that are important to today's young men. They reason that there are challenges of
other kinds requiring just as much courage as undergoing
eight weeks of boot training. Some youths will argue that
being a draft resister is far more challenging to body,
mind, and spirit than the rigors of eight weeks spent under
the thumb of a Drill Instructor who thinks you made a mistake the day you were born.

Increasingly, the Marines have found their ranks opening mainly to minority groups, Negroes and Puerto Ricans,
products of the inner-city ghettos whose educational

achievements are usually modest and whose background causes serious problems in training them once they enter the Corps. As Colonel Hallisey suggests, while the Marines prefer to have educated men in their ranks, the ranks must be filled regardless of the quality of men available. Standards, necessarily, bend.

But even the pool of available men among this country's minorities is being threatened by the same resistance to military service which affects whites, but in this case it is a resentment and resistance to white authority that causes a would-be black enlistee to hesitate. Why, asks the young black, serve in the white man's Marines? Why get stomped and kicked and shoved around in the white man's Marine Corps? Why not get the challenge of identity and self-fulfillment elsewhere—in the Black Panthers, for example?

These are the challenges that are raised now to the Marine Corps, and it seems reasonable that the Corps should examine its own soul, looking into its heretofore flawless systems of recruiting and training to see if they are, to use the term now so much in vogue, relevant to the needs of society.

But even if the Marines manage to shape their illustrious Corps to the changing mores and ideals of our society, they cannot change the basic purpose for which the Marine Corps has existed since 1775—to fight in wars.

A Marine is an infantryman.

"And because every Marine is first a rifleman, even those who will go on to such specialties as aircraft maintenance or communications perfect their marksmanship and learn the basics of infantry combat," says a Marine recruiting brochure. It offers to train a man in how to assault an enemy, how to hold his ground at any cost. At individual combat training, the brochure promises, a Marine learns the rules and tools of combat. His teachers are Vietnam veterans, and the classroom could be anything from a ten-mile stretch of beach on the southern California coast to a mock bamboo village in the forests of North Carolina. He learns fire-team, squad, and platoon tactics. He practices amphibious landings, with close air support. He becomes an airborne attacker whisked into battle by helicopter. He learns what it's like to fire an M-60 machine gun or a 3.5 rocket launcher.

These are what the Marines offer to a generation whose kinsmen sing "give peace a chance" and who wear peace buttons.

Major Charles S. Robb, son-in-law of former President Johnson, noted that the Marine Corps was not attracting as many qualified applicants as it desires. "We find the traditional appeal of service to country, or just wanting to be a Marine, is no longer sufficient," he said.

The Marine recruiter is caught in the generation gap.

Underlying the problem is the inescapable fact that in an era of increasing awareness of the rights of individuals the Marine Corps must take a civilian youth, tear down his individuality, and replace it with an esprit de corps. The ego must be subservient to the team, and that can spell trouble for both the individual and the organization.

In great frustration, a Marine asks if the Corps is supposed to make Marine training easier. Must the Corps join the rush to further permissiveness? Veteran Marines shake their heads knowingly and lament the fate of the combat team that goes into battle, not as a team, but as a gathering of willful individuals. "They'll all come back in green body bags," the veteran says grimly.

It is hard, if not impossible, for a man who rushed to join the Marines on December 7, 1941, to grasp why today's young men are reluctant to serve their country in uniform. Veterans of other wars attribute the country's youthful pacifism to cowardice, Communist subversion, laziness.

Generations of older Marines cannot understand why there should be resistance to wearing the Marine uniform today or why the traditional Marine training system is being sharply criticized.

One of the recruiters interviewed for this book, when asked to comment on the McKeon tragedy at Parris Island, said, "So what? What's the big deal, six fuckin' recruits drown? These people that complain shouldn't open their mouths unless they know the real story."

The real story, this and other Marines say, is that the world we live in is a hostile one. They see enemies beyond America's shores while at home they see a generation of young who are loathe to give up their comforts to fight to save their country. They, like Colonel Hallisey, regard the Marines as this country's last stand of individual responsibility, obligation, and service. To them permissiveness means weakness, cowardice, and collapse.

A Marine, they say, has only one job: "He fights in the duty of freedom."

Marines understand that young men join their ranks for a variety of personal reasons, some of which they may not understand themselves. It is significant to note that enlistments *rose* following publicity surrounding the McKeon "death march" of 1956. "In many ways the Marine Corps satisfies the needs of the poorly adjusted late adolescent," remarked psychologist Waldo Lyon. And Bruno Bettelheim observed, regarding presumed Presidential assassin Lee Harvey Oswald, that such youths are searching for the firm dependable father figure they have never had. In training they regress to a much younger stage of this dependency, in which their basic motivation is to please the father figure. Lyon went on to state that the Corps "provides a setting for immature youths to work through essential tasks of psychosexual development." Students of human behavior have often remarked on the undercurrent of latent homosexuality surrounding the Corps, especially in the relationship between the recruit and the Drill Instructor. In that relationship, Lyon observed in his eight years at Parris Island, "The phallic aggressive imagery used by the Drill Instructor to spur his recruits onward may help them toward focusing their sexual drives appropriately, although it is unlikely that feelings of tenderness and compassion are thus inculcated. For the insecure and uncertain, the opportunity to fondle and sleep with his rifle must be a powerful contribution toward his masculine self-image."

But another psychiatrist thought Lyon did not go far enough in his analysis of the psychosexual underpinning of the recruit-DI relationship. "I agree with your concept of phallic aggressive imagery," he wrote to Lyon, "but I think you underplay the latent homosexual relationship between the Drill Instructor and the recruit. This, incidentally, is part of many initiation rites. The initiate first has to accept the homosexual penetration by the adult before he is made a part of the adult group."

Marine boot camp *is* a severe initiation rite by which recruits qualify to join the fraternity of Marines. The boot training is a purification rite aimed at perfecting youth. "When the young man proves his manhood," observes Lyon, "he becomes self-sufficient yet interdependent with other Marines, a member of the 'Best Outfit There Is.'"

CHAPTER FOUR

BAGEL BOY

Sometime during the eight weeks of training, the exact moment I am unsure of, they painted a Jewish star on my forehead.

Private David Abrahamson

The voice of the DI crashed through the barracks.

"Abra-*ham*-son, front and *center!*"

The voice, the words, the way the Drill Instructor mispronounced his name, struck David Abrahamson with the impact of a physical assault.

He jumped from his bunk, stumbled, came up straight, and ran down the center of the squad bay toward the short, stocky, blonde crew-cut DI standing on the highly polished floor just outside the DI squad room.

"*On* the double, Abra-*ham*-son, on the *double.*"

For weeks now things had been this way, and as Private Abrahamson double-timed the length of the squad bay he was acutely aware of the rest of the platoon watching him nervously, knowing how he felt, almost feeling themselves the knots of fear that formed in his stomach and the tight breathlessness that gripped his chest. The others watched

37

in silence. This was Abrahamson's ordeal, they were thinking, not mine. Mine may be next.

The DI cocked his head toward the squad room. "Inside, Abra-*ham*-son."

It was night; the training day was over. The other DI's had gone home, leaving the platoon with Sergeant Styles. A DI always slept in the barracks, the three of them rotating the duty. Sergeant Roland Richards was the chief DI. Sergeant Donald Styles and Sergeant William Hersh were the Assistant DI's.

Private Abrahamson stood rigidly at attention in the DI squad room, waiting, as Sergeant Styles ambled slowly inside, kicking the door closed behind him. When he came around in front of Abrahamson, he squinted into the private's eyes. "Tell me somethin', Abra-*ham*-son, are you a Jew?"

"Yes, sir," Abrahamson said.

Styles nodded. "I figured you were a Jew-boy," he said, stepping across the small room to the tightly made bunk prepared by the DI's "house mouse," a scrawny Puerto Rican kid from El Barrio, East Harlem, whom the DI's had picked to do their housekeeping chores for them. Styles picked up a swagger stick from the bunk, returning to where Abrahamson stood at stiff attention. Slapping the swagger stick in his palm as he returned, the DI asked, "Jews like to eat a thing called a bagel, right, Abra-*ham*-son?"

"Yes, sir," Private Abrahamson said.

"I never did have one of those bagel things, and I don't think I ever will. I prefer *American* food."

Abrahamson said nothing. He was conscious of sweat in his palms and a sudden dryness in his throat.

"Tell me, Bagel boy, are you an old-fashioned Jew?"

Abrahamson blinked, his mind racing, trying to understand, to grasp what was happening.

"Don't just stand there, Bagel. Are you an old-fashioned Jew?"

"N-no, sir," Abrahamson said.

The DI nodded, slapping the swagger stick in his palm. "No, I guess all the old-fashioned Jews were wiped out by the Germans, eh?" He raised the swagger stick, tapping it lightly against Abrahamson's cheek, then a little harder at the side of the private's head. "Did you know Sergeant Richards is of German extraction, Abra-*ham*-son? You know what Germans think of Jews, don't you, Abra-*ham*-son?" The sergeant rapped the swagger stick against the private's head once more, then stepped away. "Get the hell outta here, Private," he barked.

Private Abrahamson moved erectly and quickly out of the squad room and back through the darkened barracks to his "rack," sinking to the bunk and hunching up his shoulders, burying his feverish face in his trembling hands.

"Oh, God," he muttered, "this is how it must have been in the concentration camps. God, how long is it going to go on?"

The question echoed in his head through the night, and when Sergeant Roland Richards' voice crackled through the predawn dark, jolting the rest of the platoon awake, Private David Abrahamson had not slept at all. Visions of awful pictures in history books of the Nazi death camps had stabbed his brain all night long while throbbing pain pulsed in his head where Sergeant Styles had tapped him with the swagger stick.

"Outta those racks, you animals," shouted Sergeant Richards, striding on long legs down the center of the bay. "Up and at 'em, shitheads."

The sergeant paused a moment, staring at Private Abrahamson as he stood by his bunk. "Get with it, Jew boy," the sergeant growled, "this ain't no fuckin' synagogue. This is the United States Marine Corps."

In March, 1969, the young Jew whom we call David Abrahamson (although that is not the name of the real boy to whom all of the incidents described in the preceding

scene allegedly happened at Parris Island, South Carolina)
went into the United States Marines after completion of
his studies at a school of business at a university in Pennsyl-
vania.

His real name is not used here because to do so would
merely perpetuate the agony that the young man has experienced and for which he was still being treated at the
time of the writing of this book. Similarly, the names of
the Drill Instructors and one witness involved in the case
of David Abrahamson have been changed for this writing
because legal proceedings growing out of the Abrahamson
case were under way at the time of the writing of this book.

David Abrahamson was twenty-one years old when he
completed college, with a dream of going on to law school.
But in order to be able to pursue his undergraduate studies
without interruption, the boy had made an arrangement to
postpone his vulnerability to military service. He had considered several of the alternatives available to these young
draft-age men, and elected to join the United States Marine
Corps Reserves. Upon completion of his college work, he
entered the Corps for basic Marine training, being sent, as
all men east of the Mississippi are, to the Marine Recruit
Training Depot, Parris Island, South Carolina.

David was both apprehensive and confident about Marine
training as he headed south to PI, as the Marines call the
world-famous island that had been home for millions of Marines through the years, Parris Island. David expected the
physical training to be difficult, but he was sure of his abilities. He'd played baseball in high school, golf in college. He
was perhaps not as strong as some men his age, but the
Marines, he knew, would build him up, and he thought that
would be good for him. He'd always been a leader in school
—active in student affairs in high school, chairman of the
interfraternity council in college. He thought he knew and
understood the requirements of leadership, and he fully ex-

pected to be able to understand why Drill Instructors acted the way they did, something which other new Marines might not so readily understand because of their limited education. And finally, David felt that any human being could bear up under any punishment so long as he knew that at a given point in time the punishment would end.

"You're a smart and sensitive boy, David," a college friend of his had said at their last meeting before David left for Parris Island, "and I'm sure you'll get along okay. Just keep your cool."

David's mother was worried, however. "I don't know why you ever wanted to go into the Marines," she said again and again. "You're much too fine, too sensitive for them. I don't see how you'll be able to bring yourself down to their level. I don't see why you should."

David listened and tried to comfort her by telling her that she always imagined the worst and the worst never happened.

But a week after his arrival at Parris Island, David Abrahamson began doubting his own words. In succeeding weeks he went through ceaseless hours of mental anguish centering on three elements of his life—that he was a college man, that he was a reservist, and that he was a Jew.

"Hey, Jew-boy," the DI's said.

"Bagel boy," they shouted.

"Hey, Bagel," they yelled.

Sergeants Richards and Styles did these things more than Sergeant Hersh, who had a Jewish-sounding name but was not a Jew.

"Just remember what we Germans think of Jews," Sergeant Richards was fond of saying.

Every third night, when Sergeant Styles slept with the platoon, David could be sure that he would be summoned to the squad bay. "Abra-*ham*-son, *front* and *center*," the Sergeant shouted, beginning the ritual. In the squad bay with the door closed, the ritual was always the same. The names, the remarks against Jews, the swagger stick in the hand. And always, the sergeant would start to slap him on the head with the stick. Soon, small deviations from the ritual appeared, until finally it included a situation where Abrahamson knelt in front of the sergeant, his back stiff, head tilted up as the swagger stick flailed the air. "Say it, Abra-*ham*-son, say it," the DI commanded.

With dry and crackling voice, the young Marine muttered, "I am crazy, I am crazy, I am crazy, I am crazy," while the DI beat the cadence of the words on the boy's head with the stick.

David Abrahamson never slept on those nights but lay tensely in his rack waiting for Sergeant Richards to barge cursing through the barracks door to get the platoon out of bed in the morning.

Each morning was the same, each day more terrible than the one before. Each moment was a tense awaiting, waiting for the next indignity, the next assault on his Jewishness. Then came the third night again and Styles summoning him to the squad room.

At some time during the eight weeks of training, the exact moment of which he would never be able to recall, he was kneeling in the squad room waiting for the ritual of the swagger stick, when the sergeant brought from his locker a small can of yellow paint and a brush. "Know what the Germans did so they could always spot the Jews?" the Sergeant asked. "They made the Jew-boys wear the Jew star on them."

At the first touch of the cold, wet paint brush on his forehead, tracing the lines between the six points of the Star of David on his sweaty skin, David Abrahamson shut his eyes and held his breath and heard, faintly in his ears, the distant roar of a million throats chanting, *"Sieg Heil, Sieg Heil, Sieg Heil, SIEG HEIL."*

The voices stopped with the first slap of the swagger stick.

"I am crazy," David Abrahamson said softly. "I am crazy. I *am* crazy. I *am* crazy. I . . . AM . . . crazy."

Graduation was three days away. David was sitting on his rack writing a letter to his family.

"What in hell you doing, Abrahamson?" asked the DI.

"I'm writing a letter," David said absently.

"You're *supposed* to be shining boots and shoes for graduation, Abrahamson," the DI said angrily.

"I haven't finished writing my letter, yet," David said.

"I think you'd better have a talk with the lieutenant, Private, 'cause, frankly, I think you've got a screw loose," the sergeant said.

The lieutenant frowned and drummed his fingers on his desk. "The sergeant is worried about you, Private. He's worried about the way you've been acting. Maybe you need some help, eh?" he asked. "From a doctor?"

"Maybe, sir," David said, his eyes wide, staring into space. His voice was strange, the words coming like an echo, without thought behind them, like a boy reciting in school while his mind was on something else far, far away.

"You go back to your area, Private," the lieutenant said. He glanced at the sergeant. "Keep your eye on him while I make a phone call, Sergeant."

Back in the squad bay, the sergeant said, "You stand by your rack, Private, facing that there wall and don't you move until *I* tell you you can."

"Yes, sir," David said.

Ten minutes later he felt someone tap him on the shoulder. "Come with me, Private," a voice said. It was not the sergeant's voice.

"I can't go anywhere until the sergeant tells me to," David said. He glanced at the man who had his hand on his

shoulder and saw a black armband on the man's uniform:
MP.

"Take him," the man with the armband said.

Others with armbands wrestled David to the floor, pulled
his arms behind his back, and snapped handcuffs on him.
Hauling him out of the barracks, the military police shoved
him into a van, making him lie face-down on the floor.

The van sped off down the company street, heading for the
Parris Island west-end medical unit, staffed with only a
minimal force because this was a Saturday. Ironically, the
Jewish Sabbath.

Sitting in the office of Navy Lieutenant Commander
Frank Forstoeffel, who had only recently completed his psychiatric residency and joined the Parris Island medical unit,
the authors, nearly a year after the mental breakdown suffered by Private David Abrahamson, were told that Abrahamson had not been seen by a psychiatrist at the Parris
Island medical unit but by a duty doctor who submitted his
diagnosis to Navy doctors at the Charleston Naval Hospital.

The report of the Navy doctors was made available to the
authors by Marine Corps Headquarters in Washington, D.C.,
and the report supported the original diagnosis of the Parris Island duty doctor on the day Abrahamson was taken
into custody, May 28, 1969. In its report, dated July 15,
1969, the Charleston Naval Hospital indicated that Abrahamson suffered acute schizophrenia and said that the
young man was emotionally distraught, had had auditory
hallucinations, was rambling in his speech, and suffered
from blocking. ("Blocking" is described as "unclear thoughts"
when the normal channels of the brain are short-circuited.)
Abrahamson was diagnosed as a paranoid type who recov-
ered quite quickly. The Navy doctors noted that the subject
had delusions about security guards and that he constantly
boasted about being able to excel in anything. In describing his condition as "overt paranoid with a schizophrenic

break," the Navy report stated that there was no psychosis and that the boy was mentally competent to handle his own affairs. This ailment, the report stated, did *not* exist prior to Abrahamson's entry into the service.

Reviewed by the Physical Evaluation Board after a period of rest and observation at the Charleston Naval Hospital, Private David Abrahamson was found unfit for further military service and was given an honorable discharge, but his ordeal was not over.

Returning home to Long Island, New York, David was put under the care of a private psychiatrist. Shocked and angered by the state of the young man's mental health, the doctor was convinced, from Abrahamson's previous medical history and the record of what happened to him in the Marines, that "the incidents at Parris Island absolutely precipitated his condition."

The doctor explained that "without the Marine Corps David Abrahamson could have gone on without any breakdown, but this kind of stress was like the straw that broke the camel's back."

The doctor ordered a series of shock treatments and hospitalization with intense observation to help David get over his "acute" reaction and his depression caused by the anti-Semitic remarks and "the whole trauma of the Corps in general."

At this time two other incidents occurred within the Marines to cause a New York Congressman to become alarmed about conditions within the United States Marine Corps. In July, 1969, there had been a series of race riots at Camp Lejeune, North Carolina, which endangered the lives of a New York Marine Reserve unit undergoing annual training at Lejeune. Reports of maltreatment of recruits from the New York area at the Parris Island Marine Corps Training Depot had also been coming in with alarming regularity. The Congressman, Mario A. Biaggi, representing the Twenty-fourth Congressional District encompassing the Bronx, decided to look into all these reports.

A Democrat, Mario Biaggi was elected in 1968, taking the seat formerly held by a Republican. Before getting into politics, Biaggi served as a lieutenant with the New York City Police Department and is the most decorated policeman in the United States (and probably the world). Referred to by newspaper headline writers as "the hero cop," Biaggi had attained a reputation as a defender and protector of the rights of policemen, stating often that men in police uniform had "become our forgotten citizens."

The stories he was receiving daily in his Bronx and Washington Congressional offices led Biaggi to believe that there were other "forgotten citizens" serving in enlisted ranks in the armed forces.

While launching an investigation into the riot at Lejeune and turning his attention to the other reports of irregularities in the U.S. Marines, Biaggi learned of the Abrahamson case. Publicly, he called for a court-martial of the two DI's involved in the Abrahamson case "for acts of bigotry against a Jewish recruit." He charged that the Abrahamson episode was not an isolated case of errant activity on the part of a pair of DI's, but was part of a general atmosphere of brutality in the Marines. "I would like to say that this case is an exception rather than the rule," he said, "but I can't honestly say that because a number of similar cases have been called to my attention."

As a member of Congress, Biaggi demanded action on the part of the Marine high command. He wrote to Corps Commandant General Leonard F. Chapman, Jr., demanding disciplinary action against the Drill Instructors accused by Abrahamson. In a reply on behalf of the Commandant, Colonel S. Fisher, Assistant Inspector General, USMC, wrote, "This Headquarters is happy to conduct an inquiry into the matter set forth in your letter and to assist your office in any way possible."

General Chapman received other mail, including an irate letter from Bernard B. Direnfeld, National Commander of the Jewish War Veterans. "Many of our members served in the Marine Corps and were exposed to the rigors and painstaking training programs that turn a raw recruit into a fighting Marine," he wrote. "Under these circumstances, there are bound to be abuses, but the allegation that individuals are singled out for abuse on the basis of religion raises wider questions concerning Marine Corps training that must be answered."

With pressures building in reaction to the publicity resulting from Biaggi's disclosure of the case of "the bagel boy," General Chapman issued a statement on December 4, 1969, in which he vowed that he would not tolerate brutality against recruits and that an investigation of the mistreatment of the Jewish Marine at Parris Island would be ordered. "The Commandant of the Marine Corps does not condone nor will he tolerate maltreatment of any Marine whatever his status," the statement concluded.

In pursuing his investigation, Biaggi raised fundamental questions touching on basic Marine Corps procedures, especially in the area of recruitment and screening of candidates for induction into the Marines. Dom Frasca, an aide to Biaggi, restated one of those questions in an interview with the authors: "Why didn't the Marines detect this boy's mental problems before they took him if, as the Marines insist, Abrahamson's mental condition preceded his induction? It isn't on his records. What they apparently did after he had his breakdown was put on his records that this mental condition preceded his induction into the Marine Corps."

For a time, Biaggi expected another Marine, a buddy of Abrahamson, Christian Young, to aid in the investigation of the case. But Christian Young began backing off from his willingness to cooperate, apparently because he was still in the Marine Reserves.

In our own investigation, we also contacted Christian Young and talked with him, but we met the same reluctance. He had, in the meantime, been contacted by a brigadier general from Marine Corps Headquarters in Washington who wanted to interrogate the young man about the case. After that, Christian flatly refused to discuss the Abrahamson case. It is interesting to conjure in one's mind the image of this young Marine reservist—a private in the Marines —sitting in a hotel room on Long Island and talking with a general officer from Washington.

We were able to talk on the telephone with Christian's mother, itself a frustrating experience and valuable in that it demonstrates the atmosphere that suddenly surrounded the disposition of the Abrahamson case after we began probing it in our research for this book:

> AUTHORS: You probably know what we're calling about.
>
> MOTHER: Well, my son's had quite a few calls since he's been home. He got a call from Washington the other day, some brigadier general or something. I know my son talked to him, and it was from Washington, that's how I knew something had started again. How did you get his name again?
>
> AUTHORS: We had information that he was a witness in the Abrahamson case.
>
> MOTHER: He really wasn't a witness. They were trying to get some information from him. Abrahamson was a friend of his in the Marines. He was in bad shape when he came home, too.
>
> AUTHORS: Your son was?

MOTHER: Quite mixed up, yeah. Once he got home and really settled down, we had hoped that was it, but then the calls started coming. All we know is that he's got six years to go in the reserve, which makes it a little rough.

AUTHORS: He was in David's platoon?

MOTHER: Right. They were friends. He had seen all the things that had been going on, but it wasn't only Dave. It seemed to be everyone. Dave it hit just a little harder.

AUTHORS: You say Chris had some problems of his own?

MOTHER: Well, he seemed quite mixed up. In fact, he didn't come right home. He happened to go to school in West Virginia before the Marines, and he was quite mixed up when he got out of the Marines and decided to go back to West Virginia, so we didn't see him for almost a month after he got out. You have to hear the stories and know what's going on to realize.

AUTHORS: What about your son now? How is he?

MOTHER: At one time he was the kind of kid, that boy, if he wasn't going to right the world nobody would. There was a time when he would have jumped right in and said "somebody's got to change this." Not any more. We heard plenty, like I said. The stories were unbelievable. I have three sons, one in the Army. They all sat and listened to what Chris said about the Marines. If it had come from anybody but him, I wouldn't have believed it.

The wheels of military justice grind slowly, and over the course of months cases such as "bagel boy" ultimately come to the kind of neat, legalistic conclusion to which they must come. If punishments are due, the military courts mete them out. Wrongdoers come before the bar to answer the charges against them, and that is as it must be, but in the end these are matters that involve a society's feelings toward itself. These are the rituals by which society convinces itself that it is against evil and dedicated to its punishment. They are exercises to ease society's conscience.

There can be no ease for David Abrahamson. There is no military court of justice that can undo what was done to his mind, nothing that a court-martial can proclaim that will erase the horrors of believing he was confined in a concentration camp, nothing that will ever restore fully his confidence that he has a grip on reality.

There is no way.

But if there is any comfort available for David Abrahamson, it is that he is alive.

Others who sought to wear the eagle, globe, and anchor emblem of the United States Marine Corps have died in the pursuit of that privilege. Thousands, of course, died in that pursuit on battlefields of honor and glory and service to the nation.

Some died in other ways.

CHAPTER FIVE

PRIVATE JOSÉ

You had a good home but you left;
You're right;
You had a good home but you left;
You're right.

Marine cadence song

A hard sun battered down on Harlem in June, 1969. The streets were like bake ovens, the air too hot to breathe, and the house too uncomfortable to stay in, even if one stripped down to shorts. Sweat soaked through José Concepción's shirt even before he reached the street after picking his way down the dim, cluttered stairway of the tenement where he lived. By the time he got downtown to the recruiting station, the shirt would be wringing wet.

Stopping for a moment on the hot sidewalk, José turned and looked up to see if his wife was at the window. She wasn't, and he didn't really expect her to be. The baby had been crying, and Dee was busy with her. Besides, there wasn't anything more to be said. José had made up his mind, explained his decision to Dee and his mother, and now he was heading downtown to make the decision final.

José was going into the Marines.

The decision, in a sense, had been made for him.

51

At age nineteen, José L. Concepción was not a boy whom anyone would especially notice in a crowd. Of medium height and weight, José was a brown-skinned Puerto Rican, the kind of kid that a New Yorker could find by the dozen pushing garment racks through clogged Seventh Avenue traffic and in the streets around Macy's in the garment district. He walked with a slight side-to-side sway that whites may have regarded as cocky but which was just youthful exuberance and a certain joy in living, in spite of the fact that life wasn't easy. He liked to get dressed up on Saturday night, wearing stovepipe trousers and his favorite blue-plaid sport coat. He didn't go in much for neckties unless Dee wanted him to wear one.

José wore no tie as he scampered down the steps into the subway for the steaming, swaying, rattling ride downtown to Marine recruiting.

This was José's second trip to the recruiter. He'd tried to join a few months earlier but failed the IQ test. He'd thought a lot about joining up that time, and when his friends on the block asked him why in hell he wanted to get into the jive-ass Marine Corps, José frowned and thought about it. But only to his closest friends did he say something about his need to show that he was a man—not a man sexually, for nobody scored better on that count than José, but in the more subtle measures of manhood: independence and toughness and the ability to see something through.

"Shit, man, who you got to prove all that to?" he was asked.

"To Dee," he said softly. "And to Mama."

Rejection by the Marines had been a blow to José, and he took a long time heading home that day, bumming around Times Square, looking in windows at the radios and record players on display. At home, Dee understood and tried to make him feel better about it.

Then a letter from José's draft board arrived telling him to report for classification.

"I don't want to go in the Army," he said, shaking his head.

"I don't see that you have much choice," Dee replied.

"Maybe I'll go down and see if the Marines'll let me take that test again," he said, more to himself than to Dee.

"Why would they do that?" Dee wondered.

José wondered, too, as the subway plunged him down the underground heart of Manhattan, leaving him off a few blocks from the recruiting station. He walked quickly to the building but went inside a little more slowly, his nervousness apparent. Explaining his situation, José sat back in a wooden chair and braced himself for the recruiter to tell him he couldn't take the test again. But the recruiter had a surprise for José.

Allowed to take the test again, José was informed that he had passed, so he didn't bother asking any questions. He didn't care anything about how the second test might have been graded, what errors might have been overlooked this time, what sort of pressure the New York recruiters might have been under to meet their quota of recruits. All that mattered to José Concepción was that now the Marines wanted him. José didn't mind the heat as much when he came outside again. He smiled and strode along the Manhattan streets with his walk of joy, no doubt causing passersby to regard him as cocky, even arrogant.

Then José began to worry. He worried about Dee and the baby, Stardell, and how they would get along without him. He would have to arrange to have his Marine pay, as little as it would be, set aside for them except just a little for him so he could have some good times. He would write to Dee every day, and he knew she would write to him. Their being in love would see to that.

José had met Dolores when he was sixteen. She was a year older. Their mothers introduced them at a family party. An attractive, dark-skinned Negro girl, Dee was full of fun, always laughing and joking and teasing him.

The two teen-agers dated often. They were married on November 5, 1966, in a church on Eighth Avenue. Neither of them was religious to the point of strict attendance at church, but they prayed together often and found a closeness in sharing their religion. They made up affectionate names for each other—Dee Dee and Wee Wee.

Refusing to allow Dee's mother to support them after their marriage, José quit school and went to work as a stock boy. Dolores took a job at the same place, leaving Stardell with her mother. Soon they had their own apartment in Harlem and tried to get along as best they could independently. There was trouble, as there always is in Harlem. Once José was mugged by a thief who hit him over the head with a steel pipe. On another occasion he became involved in an altercation with two drunken women. Their brother stormed out of the house, a gun in his hand, and shot José three times. He nearly died and carried two of the bullets in him thereafter, the doctors choosing not to risk removing them.

Even as a boy, José had had bad luck. If asked, he said the best thing that ever happened to him was winning a lifesaving medal from the Milbank Community Center in Harlem.

Then he met Dee, the second good thing to happen to him.

The Marines, he thought, would be a third. Maybe his luck *was* changing.

On June 23 José reported to the Marine receiving station at Fort Hamilton, Brooklyn, in the shadow of the spectacular Verrazzano Narrows bridge. There he was told to go home until the afternoon. Heading uptown to Harlem, José stopped and bought two Bibles, one for Dee and one for the baby. "Pray for me," he said.

The trip to Parris Island, South Carolina, is a long one, by plane and bus. A friend of José's also joined the Marines that day and traveled with him, making the journey a little more enjoyable despite their growing nervousness.

José arrived at the famous Marine Corps Recruit Training Depot on the night of June 25. The last leg of the trip was by chartered Marine bus, rattling down the single road that cuts through the marshy, sandy, palmetto-dotted tideland between Beaufort, South Carolina, and Parris Island. The bus lurched to a stop, the door swung open.

"Run, run, run, you shitheads!"

"That must be a DI," someone said in a whisper.

"You shitheads have *exactly* ten seconds to get off that mother-fuckin' bus and line up on these here marks!"

José looked out the window at rows of yellow footprints painted on the street. Scrambling with the others, he began what the Marine Corps Recruit Depot calls the "fifty-minute hour." Off the bus to the shouted obscenities from a ramrod-stiff Drill Instructor in a Smokey the Bear hat, the recruits fell into line, standing rigidly at attention, their feet in the painted footprints.

"Now you shitheads are going to *run* to that building over there," shouted the DI. "Now run, you shitheads, run."

In the next hectic minutes, José began the process of becoming a recruit. He would not be considered a Marine until he finished boot camp, eight weeks later—if he finished. In the process of becoming a recruit he would surrender the personal belongings considered unnecessary by the Marines, a DI dumping them into a wastebasket or a bag for sending home. Then, inevitably, the fastest haircut in the world—forty-five seconds, leaving the recruit as bald as clippers can make him.

Is boot camp tough? ask the Marines. Yes, they say. Can a boy make it? Millions have, they reply. Boot camp is the test.

The Marines operate boot camps at San Diego, California, and Parris Island, South Carolina. Marines in the eastern half of the United States train at Parris Island. The Recruit Training Regiment (RTR) consists of three training battalions and a Weapons Training Battalion, all located within the eight thousand acres of sand, swamp, and dry land that is Parris Island.

After checking in through the main gate, the first stop a recruit makes is Recruit Receiving, the startling introduction, already described, to the rigors that await him at Parris Island. He is immediately assigned to a platoon, which he joins several hours later. Private José Concepción was assigned to Platoon 298, E Company, 2d Battalion, RTR. The commander of the training series to which this outfit was assigned was Lieutenant Robert Harper, a man whom José would meet several times in his first two days. The officer in charge of E Company was Lieutenant Edward Trainor. The Senior Drill Instructor was Gunnery Sergeant Andrew G. Garcia. His assistants were Sergeant Terry Coles and Sergeant Clifford Callahan.

After his arrival, José followed the pattern followed by all recruits at PI. He was given an initial issue of Marine clothing—utility coat, trousers, cap, underwear, socks, and field boots. His civilian clothing was bundled to be sent home. Next came medical examinations and bucket and rifle issue. By now, José had been in the Marines two days, and he had gotten into trouble by failing to salute Lieutenant Harper and to address him as "sir." In a letter home, José was beginning to regret his decision to join the Marines, a not-uncommon feeling among recruits in their first two days. But José hinted at a more than usual harassment:

> Dear Dee,
>   I'm just writing you to tell you that I've made the biggest mistake in my life.
>   I know I've only been here for two days, but I ain't never went through shit like this before. One of the ser-

geants around here went all upside my head because I would not say sir. But in the whole I guess I can live with it. So don't worry about me and tell everybody I said hello and that I'll write them as soon as I can. I miss you and Stardell more than anything. I don't know [sic] to finally be so far away and knowing that I can't come home any time I want. I feel awful lonely, so kiss the baby and pray for me tonight.

Love,
Wee Wee

This letter was Dolores Concepción's first word that José had been beaten. His phrase "went all upside my head" was one used in ghettos to mean being beaten. But next day, José was feeling a little better, at least at the start of his letter home:

Dear Dee,

I know that you are worried about me right now, but don't be because I am doing what I'm told to do and get into as much trouble as the next man. Being here for just three days has already started to change me. But I'll tell you this much, if it wasn't for the fact that I wanted to prove something to you and my mother, and especially my mother, and damn near everyone else, Dee, I would've left this place the first day here. I've been going through hell. You see, it's like this. They want me to learn everything in a minute and keep it in my head and you know I can't keep to [sic] many thing in it. But in the whole everything is okay. The food is not as bad as some people claim it is. But then again I can eat anything. I still eat like all hell but I do miss being with you Dee and tasting some of your cooking. It would seem when I was home all I wanted to do was go around the block and stay out all night but if I was home right this minute I would be with you and Stardell and I do hope she misses me a little bit. Give her a kiss for me and if anything happen over there let me know. I love

you Dee Dee with all of my heart so take good care of
yourself because when I come back I'm coming back a
man and not a coward. . . . Saying goodbye,

Love,
Wee Wee

Two companions stay with a man in the first days of
Marine boot camp, as, indeed, they do in training posts in
all the services—loneliness and fear. The boy away from
home for the first time gets homesick, of course, but Private
José was apparently having more than these usual difficulties.
One of the Assistant Drill Instructors assigned to Platoon
298, Sergeant Terry Coles, a soft-spoken young Negro, said,
"At first he seemed like an average recruit, but as a few
hours or a day or so went by, he proved to be less than the
average-type recruit. Some of them can go along with the
change in atmosphere, some of them can't. Obviously, he
couldn't."

Sergeant Coles remembers that José was slow in getting
up in the morning. "His reason was because he wasn't used
to getting up early in the morning," Coles explained.

Coles said he never struck José and denied any knowledge of anyone else striking him. Sergeant Coles affirms that
José was troublesome: "He more or less didn't want to go
along with the program. He was the type of recruit who
seemed to have a mental block toward recruit training or
authority. He wasn't used to it and didn't want to go along
with it." He added that there was nothing that could be
done to make José conform.

There was something that could be done, however. A
special training unit known as the Motivation Platoon
has been established at Parris Island to handle special
cases, whether they be recalcitrants, overweight men, or
others requiring special training. A recruit may be referred to "Motivation" for an hour, a day, or however long
it takes to shape him up. Coles says to his knowledge Concepción was not sent to "Motivation."

He was sent, however, although José thought he was being sent to the brig. Undoubtedly, José had some reason to believe he might be going to the brig. DI's often tell recruits that they'll go to jail if they don't soon shape up, and José heard threats of this nature. He alludes to going to the brig in the following letter, although he was never destined for it:

> Dear Dee,
>   I just want to tell you that I might not be here for long because I might go back home or go to the brig for a week or two. But don't worry and I hope you won't be mad at me if I come back home. I tried my best to do right, but it's just not going to work. I know everybody is going to be disappointed in me, but I don't give a hell. All I want to do is get the hell out of here. I'm sorry, Dee, but that's the truth. I'm not going to let them hit me like I was an animal or something and I don't like nobody putting hands on me. So me and my Senior Drill Instructor had it out and he wants me to get the hell out of here. So I don't give a damn. I'll write you more when I can tell what happens.
>
> Love,
Wee Wee

It was not to the brig, although José believed so, but to the Motivation Platoon that he was sent. There is a considerable difference. The brig is a jail, of course, while Motivation is simply an intensified training program consisting mainly of running around the base again and again. Either would have been enough to further demoralize José, whose treatment at Parris Island had been beyond the bounds the Marine Corps sets for the handling of recruits.

Although a considerable amount of harassment and even rough handling is commonplace and somewhat necessary in Marine training at Parris Island, José Concepción was treated to more than the usual amount before he was sent to Motivation.

At Parris Island the Drill Instructor is king. His first words to his recruits are likely to be along this line: "You guys may not like it here, but don't go sneaking any letters off to your Congressmen. All those letters have to be approved by headquarters—and be careful what you write to the folks at home if you don't want to get into trouble. I don't want to hear a lot of stuff about your rights. You ain't got no rights. You're recruits. The Drill Instructor is God. You're shitheads."

To youths already lonely and scared, those words are menacing. The Marines do not officially censor mail, although the implication in the DI's words is that they do. The DI's chief weapon in shaping boys into Marines is his power and their fear of it. The recruit is told again and again that he is the lowliest thing on the face of the earth. Throughout training, recruits might be slapped, slugged, and kicked for small mistakes. The purpose of all of this harassment is to tear down the individual personality that has come into the Marine ranks and to rebuild it, fashioning the boy into a tough, proud, and daring fighting man. The purpose, too, is to find out which men will withstand the treatment and which will break.

But the line between rough training and brutality is hard to define, and too often it is crossed.

José Concepción had more than his share of rough treatment at the hands of DI's. His letters testify to that. He was a strong-willed, rebellious recruit. The decision to send him to Motivation is evidence of that. Although he again referred to going to jail, he meant Motivation when he wrote to his sister, "To tell you the truth I'm getting myself in a lot of trouble. Today I'm supposed to be going to the brig (jail) house for not doing what I'm told to do. And I just don't care anymore." To Dee, he wrote, "Don't be mad at me but I think I'm going to go to (brig) jail and I don't know for how long. I'm supposed to be going today. I guess I came down here with the wrong attitude or something."

On July 1, José was transferred to the Motivation Platoon. Even before he was completely processed into the platoon, he disappeared, officially listed as an unauthorized absence. For Parris Island MP's he was the 736th "military police lookout" since the beginning of 1969.

Four days later his body was found by some women Marines along Ballast Creek, some two miles from the Motivation Platoon barracks.

Dr. William Manning, a Navy physician, found in his cursory examination of the body that there were swellings around the facial area which could have been the result of an assault or beating. Dr. Manning made only a superficial examination of the body, assuming that the boy had died by drowning. He stated that it was "hard to tell if there were any lacerations on the body because of the decomposition" of it. He did not undress the body, which was clad in the recruit uniform and boots, certainly far too heavy to be worn if someone was trying to swim the creek. The swelling in the face, Dr. Manning felt, could have been caused by the nibbling of crabs and shrimp. He concedes, however, that the "swelling of the face may have been caused by a fight." The doctor did not touch the skull in any way to determine if it had been injured. It was up to a Navy pathologist or the commanding officer to order an autopsy. Neither one did.

Roger Pinckney, the Beaufort County Coroner, who is not a physician, ruled that José died of accidental drowning. Marine Form N, a death certificate, was signed by Captain Manning. It was also signed by Dr. John Egan, who did not view the body.

In a closed and sealed casket, José Concepción's body was returned to his wife for burial.

Dolores Concepción refused to believe that José, an excellent swimmer, had drowned accidentally. Her demands for an investigation of the death led to a month-long Marine Corps probe that concluded that José had indeed drowned. The Marines said, "If Mrs. Concepción has in her possession some material or information that she thinks would lend some credence to her allegations, then, of course, we would be happy to receive it and reopen the case."

Mrs. Concepción, having only José's letters, called radio station WINS and asked to talk to Dick Levitan. Examination of the letters and Mrs. Concepción's account of her husband's ability as a swimmer raised serious doubts about his death. She was advised to get in touch with Congressman Mario A. Biaggi, of the Bronx, while the Concepción case was made the subject of a special radio report on the station. The investigation of the death of Concepción was reopened with a Biaggi-Levitan visit to Parris Island.

That investigation indicated that the Concepción case had not been thoroughly investigated by the Marines. Questions put to the highest officers at the Marine base indicated that they had little accurate knowledge of the case, were confused over certain facts about it, and were more interested in glossing over the situation than they were in satisfactorily concluding it.

On asking to be shown the location at which Concepción's body had been found by the women Marines, Biaggi was told that the corpse was found at one location while another Marine officer was informing Levitan that the body had been found at another spot, some distance away. The discrepancy was clear evidence that the top officers of Parris Island had not conducted a very thorough review of the case themselves but had simply accepted the reports of lower officers as to what happened to Concepción.

The commanding officer of Parris Island, Major General Oscar F. Peatross, tried unsuccessfully to keep Levitan from accompanying Biaggi on the tour of the base. Then, to be sure that no base personnel were caught unaware of their presence, the general ordered their automobiles preceded wherever they went on the base by another vehicle with flashing lights and siren.

On another occasion, Levitan was actually locked in an office in an effort to separate him from Biaggi.

This tour of the base and interviews with officers and men about the Concepción case answered none of the questions that had been raised about the fate of Private José.

Returning to Washington, Biaggi wrote to the Commandant of the Marine Corps, General Leonard F. Chapman, Jr. Biaggi informed the general of his visit to Parris Island and of his inquiry into the Concepción death. "Based on the information given to me by senior officers, it is my strong belief that an autopsy should be performed in order to conclusively establish the cause of the boy's death," Biaggi wrote.

To the press, Biaggi stated, "There were important omissions in the investigation. The present findings, therefore, can only be considered inconclusive." Among the items which Biaggi considered important but which the Marine investigation did not sufficiently cover were the facts that the body was fully clothed in long trousers, a short-sleeved shirt, and heavy combat boots; that Concepción had a reputation as an excellent strong swimmer; and the charges in his letters that he had been beaten by his Drill Instructors. "None of that was considered," Biaggi charged. He was also bothered by the Marine Corps's refusal to allow the next of kin to view the body. "That bothers me, but not half as much as those boots. They are puzzling. Why would anyone attempt to swim that creek with huge, heavy boots on his feet? It doesn't make sense."

Because José Concepción's remains were legally in the hands of the family, further examination of the body to determine the exact cause of death became a matter for the family and the courts of New York. Biaggi and Mrs. Concepción filed papers in Kings County court to have the body exhumed. Appearing before Judge Hyman Korn, Biaggi asked for a show-cause order directing the Cemetery Association of the City of New York, the Evergreen Cemetery in Brooklyn, where José was buried, the City Board of Health, and the city medical examiner's office to appear before the judge in a hearing into the petition. Judge Korn set the date for the hearing as October 10.

In her petition to the court, Mrs. Concepción stated her belief that the body "contained certain wounds, certain markings, and certain punctures and other indications of a beating which said marks could not have been caused by drowning." She stated that her request for an autopsy before the burial of the body had been refused and that her attempts to obtain information on the cause of her husband's death had been "fruitless and the replies to Petitioner's requests have been vague and unresponsive."

Biaggi told the court of his investigation into the death and his conversations at Parris Island with Drill Instructors, examining physicians, and others which led him to conclude that because of "the many suspicious circumstances surrounding the death of this young boy an obligation was owed to the wife and child of the deceased and to the community at large to conduct an autopsy so as to accurately determine the cause of death."

Three months after the death, Judge Korn granted the application for exhumation of the body. In that time, the body had been in water for four days, had been only partially embalmed, and had been interred.

Dr. Milton Helpern, the city's chief medical examiner, supervised a complete autopsy on October 30, almost four months to the day after José Concepción died. Conducting the autopsy was Dr. Michael M. Baden, associate medical examiner. Their report "did not disclose any findings of a cause of death other than the one certified without autopsy by the military authorities."

But the report pointed out that the "advanced postmortem decomposition prior to the discovery of the body and also since the date of burial have obscured the usual findings that can be observed in a death by drowning in a fresh autopsy or in a well-embalmed body."

And then the New York medical examiners gave what, in effect, was a lecture to the military on how to handle its corpses:

> The frustration of attempting to determine the cause and manner of death in a poorly embalmed body should make clear the importance of the performance of a complete autopsy in a case of this type, at the time the body is found. There should not be any room for speculation as to the cause of an unexpected death of an apparently young healthy adult.

The only conclusive finding in the October 30 autopsy report was that there was no evidence "of fresh traumatic injury," meaning that José *might not* have been beaten to death. But it does not mean that José wasn't beaten or that he drowned accidentally, as the Marine Corps maintains.

What, then, happened to Private José?

We know only that the day he went to Motivation he disappeared. Eleven days after he had set foot on Parris Island, South Carolina, he was dead, leaving his wife only a handful of letters in which he claimed that he was beaten regularly by his Drill Instructors. These beatings made him desperate to get away. It may be that he was so desperate that he did indeed foolishly try to swim the treacherous tide waters of Ballast Creek with the heavy burden of uniform and combat boots. Perhaps his battered face was the result of four days in the water and the nibbling of shrimp and crabs.

The only certainty is that Private José Concepción died at Parris Island Marine Training Depot, that he said he had been maltreated prior to his death, and that his remains were ineptly handled, so that the exact cause of his death can never be known.

Had his been the only case of alleged beatings, undue harassment, and other abuses at Parris Island, José Concepción's death would not have provoked the fundamental questions that it does, indeed, raise. Another recruit died under similar circumstances only two days before José's body was discovered.

Those questions are ones the Marine Corps, for its own good, must answer. Is it true, as seems probable, that sadistic brutality has governed Parris Island for years? Is there reason for parents to wonder, when they read of deaths due to drowning or pneumonia or influenza, if those are really the reasons? Is brutality wrecking morale and patriotism in the very men that are expected to draw upon morale and patriotism in this country's time of need? Are we training and toughening our Marines, or are we maltreating them, making them bitter, and undermining the loyalty we will surely expect of them? These questions should trouble the Marines as much as they trouble us.

Marine Commandant Chapman summed it up well in a speech to the New York Union League, January 22, 1970. He said a Marine "knows there is a huge difference between discipline and brutality. He knows that without discipline his unit will fail in combat, and if his unit fails, he and his friends will die. And he also knows that when discipline breaks down, brutalization sets in."

It would be easy and comfortable to say that the death of José Concepción and the brutalized mind of David Abrahamson are exceptions.

They are not.

CHAPTER SIX

THE DI

We have been living under that ghost since 1956.

A Marine DI

A straight-backed, glaring, roaring, hard-nosed, hard-faced, swagger-sticked, obscenity-shouting, combat-tested, discipline-minded, tough, bellow-lunged, lean-legged, flat-bellied son of a bitch, a Marine Drill Instructor *will* make a Marine out of a recruit and a team out of seventy-five assorted individuals that, as far as he is concerned, will be "the best goddamned platoon that ever came out of boot camp."

To do this, he will use every means available, make no apologies for using them, and resent any insinuation that what he is doing is cruel or mean or inhuman or brutal. A man on a battlefield who has not been previously tested for his endurance to cruelty, meanness, inhumanity, and brutality will not survive, and survival is what the Marine Drill Instructor is concerned with.

"Look at this shithead," a DI barks to a platoon of recruits, his lean and leathery face hard against the chin-in and at-attention face of a raw recruit who has done something wrong. "Look at this shithead, because this man is the one who will get your ass *killed* in Vietnam!"

67

Yet the Drill Instructor at Parris Island does not have the mission of training a man for combat. His job is to lay a foundation of discipline and obedience on which others in the Corps will build skills that a man must take with him into combat. "The concept of the Drill Instructor is that of a man who transforms a raw civilian into a basic Marine. As far as training him for combat, this is not his mission," explained Master Sergeant Peter Frano, a Marine recruiter with four years of experience as a Parris Island DI. "The DI trains the individual to the point of getting him to follow orders, to do what he's told to do, to work as a team, a unit. If a man cannot work as part of a team or follow orders, then he won't be able to perform his duties in combat. But to say that a man is combat-trained at Parris Island is a falsehood, and this is not the job of the DI, to make him a combat Marine."

Maltreatment of recruits by Drill Instructors during this process is strictly forbidden and officially condemned by the Marine Corps.

"There is an order, not just a guide, but a Regimental Order that tells a DI what he can do and what he can't do," states Master Sergeant William G. Stiles, chief instructor of the Parris Island Drill Instructors School.

On the other hand, psychologist Waldo Lyon, for eight years the chief psychologist at Parris Island, contends that physical maltreatment of recruits is a normal part of the severe Marine initiation rite and is subtly condoned, although officially prohibited, by the Corps.

Unfortunately, the psychologist is correct.

Maltreatment of recruits at Parris Island and other Marine Corps training bases is a fact of life, and the perpetrator of this maltreatment, which in many cases is too gentle a description, is the Marine DI. Over a recent forty-five-month period, fifty-eight Parris Island DI's were court-martialed on charges of maltreatment, and thirty-four of them were convicted. A considerable number of the cases occurred in 1969. Parris Island is not alone, however. Between January 1 and October 15, 1969, at the Marine Recruit Depot at San Diego, California, two general courts-martial were held for DI's accused of maltreatment, as well as seven special courts-martial on the same charge, one summary court-martial for maltreatment, and one for illegal financial dealings. In this same period, ten recruits died at San Diego for a variety of reasons, none of them, according to the Marine Corps, as a result of the crimes for which DI's were tried, although the cases reported bear striking similarities to deaths due to "medical causes" so often listed on death certificates at Parris Island.

The rising incidence of cases of maltreatment has created some public interest, but not nearly so intense as that which followed the McKeon "death march" of 1956.

"I can tell you that this furor today is nothing like it was back then," says Dr. Paul Sayres, a civilian in the Parris Island neuropsychiatric branch. He attributes the increases in numbers of maltreatment cases to periods of national stress such as that which developed throughout the 1960's. Before World War II, he says, there were few maltreatment courts-martial. The number increased during the war, then declined in the postwar period. It rose again during the Korean War. Then came the McKeon case and intense public scrutiny of the Corps, resulting in a sharp decrease in cases. The onset of the Vietnam war triggered another upward trend in maltreatment cases because of the considerable pressure applied to the Corps to feed men into the Vietnam pipeline.

Although every DI at Parris Island is aware of the McKeon "death march" and its effect on the Corps, this awareness has not made DI's less brutal or less inclined to be unnecessarily tough. Rather, the DI's resent being reminded of McKeon. "We have been living under that ghost since 1956," one DI complained.

The wife of a Drill Instructor accused of maltreatment in the case of the "bagel boy" also spoke with resentment against criticism of DI treatment of recruits. "I think it's a damned shame that they send these little babies down here for somebody to straighten out and when somebody tries to straighten them out, they can't touch them. How are they going to discipline them?"

The wives and families of Marine Drill Instructors provide an interesting subject for further study by the sociologist or psychologist. They do not, apparently, lead the hard life that has occasionally been described as one of rootlessness and wandering after the father-husband from post to post, base to base. Waldo Lyon and L. L. Oldaker have made some studies of the child, the school, and the military family and concluded that such children live in an intact home with a firm father holding down a job. They also live in a community sharing many goals and anxieties. If the family moves to another military housing area, the new community and school welcome the child as smoothly as possible. There are negative aspects, however, and these include the fact that the family may live in an isolated area with schools of uneven quality. School may be interrupted at any time of the year. Intermittent father absence may occur at critical times in a child's development. This may be especially true of the DI who will sleep with his platoon every third night. Marine families maintain a cohesiveness even after they have been separated from the Marines. Matthew McKeon, now living quietly in Massachusetts, is surrounded in his neighborhood by several other former-Marine families.

While on active duty, the Marine who is the head of a family puts into practice with his own children his "habitual explanation that adolescent maladjustment results from lack of discipline." Thus he may function appropriately as a firm father, but often his excessively harsh discipline becomes counterproductive.

Marines tend to marry women who admire their precepts, studies have found, so both the Marine husband and the wife will tend to be harsh with their children, especially in the area of school development.

The Marine DI is acutely aware of the Corps's stress on improving one's education—all career Marines are officially encouraged to pursue their studies. Lyon found that in a group of 121 career Marines, 38.8 per cent had completed the high school equivalency test in the service, in addition to 40.5 per cent who had previously finished high school.

These same 121 career Marines provided some other interesting statistics that throw some light on the character of the man who chooses to be a Marine all his life. A man who joins a Corps of career Marines finds that those Marines have a background suggesting adolescent rebellion and/or family disintegration. Lyon's study of the 121 career Marines showed that "26.4 per cent reported their parents separated or divorced, and 59.5 per cent had failed to graduate from high school, prior to their enlistments. For many of these men, the Marine Corps provided a 'last chance' opportunity which they have accepted totally."

In so doing, they have accepted the whole of Marine Corps culture, including the acceptance of violence as a part of Marine life. Dr. Marvin Wolfgang suggests an inquiry into "the so-called legitimate but inconspicuous use of force and how it brutalizes society." It has been suggested that the National Commission on the Causes and Prevention of Violence study the United States Marine Corps to learn about institutionalized violence. It is also suggested strongly by many that the Marines drop their pretense that violence is not condoned.

The Marine official policy is quite explicit: "Maltreatment is construed to include any form of assault, regardless of the degree of force used; or imposing directly or indirectly any form of abusive or oppressive treatment; or imposing directly or indirectly excesses in physical exertion or activity. The threat of any of these acts, even without physical action, may also be considered maltreatment."

These acts are punishable by Article 93 of the Uniform Code of Military Justice.

"But somebody's got to touch him," insists General Peatross, commanding officer of Parris Island. "Some of these kids just lie down and fold up on you, and then somebody's got to touch them. That's what Melson did—just stretched out on the floor on his face."

Nobody argues with the fact that a DI may have to touch a recruit to assist him, although in the Melson case, as shown, the recruit had been maltreated and it was the maltreatment that made it necessary for him to be assisted.

The only lawful touching of a recruit is to adjust his position or uniform or to save him from injury or death. It is one of the least obeyed regulations on the Marine Corps books.

"For every DI who is court-martialed, there are a dozen who do the same thing or maybe worse and never get reported," a Marine corporal claimed. There is hardly a Marine to be found who cannot recount tales of maltreatment that went unpunished. The great bulk of maltreatment episodes go unreported and unpunished.

Colonel Robert J. Perrich, commander of the Recruit Training Regiment at PI, says, "If we hear about it, we go after it."

Hearing about it is the problem.

It would be expected that chaplains would hear about it, and they do. There is at least one case on record of a Catholic chaplain newly assigned to Parris Island who spent several hours a week listening to recruits at confession. The chaplain suffered a nervous breakdown and was transferred from PI.

The communication of tales of maltreatment to chaplains is not encouraged. Lyon told a meeting of psychologists and psychiatrists:

> There are many subtle communications condoning maltreatment. A chaplain preached a sermon advocating that recruits report maltreatment; the battalion commander implied such matters were not in the province of the chaplin. Light sentences for conviction for maltreatment offenses contrast with heavy sentences for conviction for other offenses. A sergeant was convicted of assaulting a number of recruits, choking one and inflicting a broken jaw, a broken nose, and a cut lip on three others. His only punishment was reduction in grade three ranks, but one-third of this punishment was suspended. Other carefully prepared cases fell apart when recruits denied on the witness stand their earlier sworn statements. These maltreatment offenses are not confined to the "maladjusted"—one particularly outstanding Drill Instructor, given recognition in a national magazine, was later relieved of duty for maltreatment. Many a Drill Instructor uses maltreatment dispassionately in his armamentarium of leadership tactics and is not necessarily more "sadistic" than the next Marine.
>
> In an effort to solve this maltreatment problem, assistance of the psychiatric unit was requested to psychiatrically screen Drill Instructor candidates. Extensive follow-up studies of this psychiatric screening revealed it to be totally ineffective in predicting who would later be relieved of duty for maltreatment. However, the Marine Corps insisted on the psychiatric stamp of approval on the prospective Drill Instructors, and the final negative report of research was blocked from reaching the desk of the commanding general.
>
> Efforts to set up a background and personality inventory to identify potentially unsuccessful Drill Instructors showed that Drill Instructors likely to be relieved of duty tended to be glib, superficial manipulators who were skill-

ful at selecting the "right answer" on a personality inventory. It was very difficult to psychiatrically disqualify a well-motivated career Marine on this type of negative evidence. When violence is institutionalized in a society, its perpetrators do not evidence strikingly distinguishing personality characteristics.

"*Why* should anyone want to be a Drill Instructor?" asks Gunnery Sergeant Ed Evans in an article in *Leatherneck,* the Corps's official magazine (the *only* magazine published for public consumption by a branch of our armed services). "The reasons are many, and range from personal to professional. The point is that every DI is on the drill field because he has a reason for wanting to be there."

The reasons do vary from DI to DI. Some earnestly believe that they owe something to the Corps, and that by training new Marines they are paying back something to the Corps. Staff Sergeant David Stott, a DI at Parris Island who was accused of maltreatment of a recruit, spoke of his philosophy as a DI. "It is stated in the pledge that all Drill Instructors take prior to becoming a Drill Instructor: indoctrinate him into the love of Corps and country."

As indoctrinators of a special creed, the United States Marines are exceeded by few, if any, other groups. The DI pledge that puts love of Corps ahead of love of country is a philosophy that pervades the Marines. "For Corps and country" is the slogan, and always in that order. *Semper Fidelis* —always faithful—applies in the same sequence to Corps and country. This indoctrination is swift and sure in most cases.

One of the men interviewed for this book on the day he joined the Marines in New York City was interviewed again at Parris Island two weeks into his boot training. The total acceptance of the Marine philosophy is apparent: "I like it right now. It's hard, but I like it. They're strict. The Marine Corps is based on discipline. If you can take orders, sir, you can make it in the Marine Corps, sir. In our platoon there's only a few that don't give a damn. Sooner or later they'll get rid of them and we'll have a good platoon."

For every seventy-five to eighty recruits, there are three DI's on whom the Corps depends to instill respect and obedience to Corps and country—the Drill Instructor and two Assistant Drill Instructors. One of these men will be with the platoon at all times. Normally, they rotate their duty, each man sleeping with the platoon every third night while the other two DI's spend twelve to fourteen hours a day with the men in the course of training. With these three men, each recruit starts even. All are equal.

"The DI that trains them never sees them the way they come in here," explained General Peatross. "It wouldn't be too good if they saw the way some of these kids come in here, pretty horrible-looking sights when they come in. By the time the DI gets them, they all look the same. They spend a period of time with their DI's before they actually enter training, two, three, or four days."

"During the first week you look for the problem privates," explained Sergeant Ronnie Reichert, a DI accused of maltreating a recruit. Reichert is twenty-four years old, has been in the Marines six years, and has served one tour of duty in Vietnam. Scheduled for a second tour, he found that his rotation back to Vietnam was delayed, partly because of the accusations against him, partly because he was regarded as an outstanding DI. Describing the initial period he spends with recruits, he said, "I just look for the privates that shouldn't be there to begin with, that have slipped by the recruiters, the ones that aren't going to make it because of physical reasons."

Ultimately, these recruits, if they turn out to be the "problem privates" the DI suspects they will be, will be sent to Motivation or to one of the other special training sections on the island. Reichert says that in the first week, recruits are not referred to these special units. "You can't use Motivation because you don't know for sure yet about the recruit. Just because a private is unaccustomed or he just doesn't know yet, you can't send him to Motivation, not during the first week." He states that recruits are sent to Motivation only on the approval of commissioned officers.

Once a man is sent to the Motivation Platoon, he is, in almost all cases, permanently out of the original DI's hair. "Usually they are out there so long," says Sergeant Reichert, "that it's just about impossible for them to catch up. They try to place these privates in platoons that are at the same day of training that these privates were in when they left."

The Marine Corps states confidently that it is the existence of the Motivation Platoon—known officially as the Special Training Branch—that makes it unnecessary for a DI to maltreat a recalcitrant or problem recruit. "A Drill Instructor doesn't have to resort to physical abuse if he has problems with a boy," Colonel Perrich stated. "He can simply send him over to STB and let them handle it."

The director of STB, Major John Murphy, added, "If we can't handle it, we call for the military police. We don't believe that maltreatment ever makes a better Marine out of anybody. If we can't do anything with them, then they are discharged."

Here, then, is a situation in which the DI's say they have no cause to maltreat a recruit because they can send a man to Motivation, the STB officers say they have no need to maltreat a man because they can call the MP's, and the MP's say they don't mistreat recruits, either, because they can pass a recruit on to someone else who can discharge him or court-martial him, leaving him to the Marines in the brig (a fate that is discussed in following chapters), where, by Marine testimony, no one is maltreated either.

"The mistreatment of any person, particularly one as

vulnerable as the recruit," say the Parris Island Standards of Conduct in dealing with recruits, "is an act of poor leadership and of disloyalty to the Corps and this regiment."

Putting it another way, Major Henry W. Austin, director of the Drill Instructor School at Parris Island, said, "The basics that this school teaches are an absolute requirement for an NCO, because he's in the people business."

Learning "the people business" at the PI Drill Instructors School is a seven-week undertaking that will conclude with the Marine NCO adding to his service record Military Occupation Specialty 8511—Drill Instructor, entitling him to wear the brown Smokey the Bear hat, symbol of the DI.

Since the school began operating in October, 1952, it has graduated more than 5,400 DI's. The school contends that not all men who attend the school graduate. One class began with ninety-six members, it was reported, and at the end of the course "fifty-two of the best were graduated."

The DI School comes under the command of Colonel Perrich, commanding officer of the Recruit Training Regiment. On the staff of the school director are a chief instructor, seven DI's, one administrative assistant, and a maintenance NCO. With this staff the school offers potential DI's eleven subjects covering all aspects of recruit training.

For the school, men with the minimum rank of corporal and minimum age of twenty-one are sought, and according to a Marine source, these men are evaluated by a screening team consisting of one field-grade officer from the Recruit Training Regiment and three DI's with the rank of gunnery sergeant. They evaluate a candidate for the school to determine his ability to maintain self-control under stress; his reliability; any signs of immaturity, negligence, indebtedness, and family problems; his potential and ability for handling troops; and his proficiency in his

MOS (Military Occupation Specialty). By these standards, the Marine Corps contends, it sifts out all but the best, citing one case in which only sixty-eight men out of nine hundred candidates were eventually selected for and graduated from the school.

These men, therefore, are, by Marine Corps estimates, the cream of the crop, a fact that underscores the seriousness of any charge of maltreatment on the part of any DI.

The allure of being counted among the best is one reason why Marine NCO's apply for DI status. That DI's have an "unusual opportunity to earn promotions" is another incentive. Additionally, all DI's assigned to recruit platoons are furnished free laundry and dry cleaning of their uniforms, an ample supply of which is issued to them at the start of their assignments.

Once assigned to a platoon, the DI can avail himself of the services of a recruit known as "the house mouse," one of a few nicknames that DI's are permitted to use under the Parris Island regulations on treatment of recruits. "He makes up the Drill Instructor's bunk and he cleans the Drill Instructor's office," explained Sergeant Stott, "and we have what is called the 'admin body' or the 'scribe,' who helps with the administrative paper work."

The working day for the DI begins early, earlier than the recruit day. Long before dawn, the DI's, spit-and-polish perfect, march to their platoons, joining the one DI who has slept the night in the "barn" with the "animals." The rigorous training day begins.

It begins with the indescribable authority of a DI voice cutting through the morning dark, startling sleeping recruits awake, and setting the cadence for a day that will be dominated by the ceaseless sound of a DI voice. The impact of that voice is almost physical. The words it speaks are drawn from an incredible lexicon of profanity.

The Marine Corps specifically forbids the use of profane and obscene language:

> A practice to be eliminated is that of directing vulgarity and profanity toward recruits. A Drill Instructor who must interlace his remarks to a recruit with a constant stream of vulgarity and verbal filth will not be tolerated. Such a Drill Instructor demonstrates his own lack of self-confidence when he has to assert himself against a defenseless recruit by profane language. A Drill Instructor who must bury his words of instruction in a stream of senseless profanity is at a loss for words to express himself; he reduces the value of his instruction and mars the image of the noncommissioned officer which he projects to his recruits; and he teaches recruits that profanity is expected and accepted in the Marine Corps. Drill Instructors will not direct toward recruits vulgar, obscene, or profane language.

"That," said a Marine veteran with a wry smile, "is a lot of bullshit."

Drill Instructors can and will recite the SOP (standard operating procedure) on use of profanity, knowing full well that the SOP on vulgarity is not worth the paper it's mimeographed on.

"Are you allowed to swear at a recruit?" we asked Sergeant Stott.

"No, sir."

"How do you feel about a DI that does swear at a recruit?"

"Sir, you've got to realize that we are only human. We're not superhuman beings. There are times, I'm sure, that when you yourself get aggravated, when you are under pressure, that you don't always use the Queen's English. I don't say that I don't swear, or that I haven't."

Rare, indeed, is the DI who doesn't or hasn't.

The SOP that bans profanity bans a host of other

practices, most of which have been used by Drill Instructors at one time or another. If they haven't been used, one wonders why they are included in the SOP. The list of "examples" of maltreatment banned by the Corps includes: slapping, kicking, biting, pinching, hitting, or otherwise assaulting a recruit, or causing any other person to do the same to a recruit. For instance, "the cutting, scraping, abrading, stepping on, or in any other way abusing recruits' trigger fingers so as to make them more sensitive for squeezing the rifle trigger properly constitutes maltreatment."

Also banned is hazing, a few examples of which are included in the SOP: participating in blanket parties, taking part in belt lines, exercising to exhaustion, conducting guerrilla exercises, running unauthorized relays, assuming Chinese thinking position, swallowing too much food or drink, eating paper or other nonfoods, smoking under a blanket, bathing with sand, shaving dry, sleeping on decks, crouching in a wall locker, working under a bunk, standing in a corner, packing and unpacking several times, collecting a bucket of steam, sewing pockets shut, placing a bucket on the head, opening a rifle bolt with nose, scrubbing deck with toothbrush, reading mail aloud, delivering useless messages, waiting senselessly.

The larcenous collection of money from recruits, long a tawdry tradition among DI's in Marine boot camps before the McKeon furor, has been banned.

The standards of conduct in dealing with recruits is a six-page, single-spaced document, a list of do's and don'ts, most of which are *still done*.

Manhandling recruits is known as "thumping," and not all recruits think it's a bad practice. Speaking to a reporter who toured Parris Island in the period immediately after the death of José Concepción, another seventeen-year-old Bronx, New York, boy said, "I got thumped. Most of us did, but I'm not griping. It was good for us. My

Drill Instructor explained it all. You have to be tough. Got to learn to take the punishment. I'm a better man for it. I learned not to be afraid of my Drill Instructor, and now I'm not afraid of anybody in the whole damned world."

Still another recruit at this time said with a kind of fatalism, "Maltreatment is as indigenous to the U.S. Marine Corps as cactus is to the desert."

All recruits expect to be "thumped." All Drill Instructors know that "thumping," while officially banned, will be overlooked.

Fear remains the DI's chief weapon, however. A DI explained, "We completely break down their ego. Then we motivate them, very slowly building them back up into what we want them to be, Marines. If they build up too fast or too much, then we break them back down. We lower the boom."

If a platoon starts to show too much spirit or cockiness, the DI feels it's his duty to bring down their enthusiasm. "As far as I'm concerned," says a DI in this situation, "tomorrow they ain't gonna do nothin' right."

Lance Corporal H. G. Harrison, twenty-one years of age, reflected on his boot camp days as he flew home, on his way toward a discharge after having served thirteen months in Vietnam. "I was trained to be an animal," he said, "but being an animal in Vietnam saved my life. Maybe I've been brainwashed, but all in all, I think the Marines helped me face the world. It's a cold, cruel world, and if you can't be strong enough, you won't make it. When I was a kid, I didn't think I was going to make it. But now I know I can and I will."

In all likelihood, the Marine Corps helped Harrison achieve what he would not have achieved had he not faced the rigors of Boot camp and the experience of being transformed at the hands of a Drill Instructor. But not everyone is as fortunate. Some people are born losers, and losers, in the Marines, have a rough road.

CHAPTER SEVEN

BLACK, WHITE, AND GREEN

I do not believe that the recent events are typical.

General Leonard F. Chapman, Jr.

On July 6, 1969, the Second Battalion, 25th Marines, 4th Marine Division, a reserve unit from Garden City, Long Island, New York, arrived at Camp Lejeune, North Carolina, for two weeks of routine summer training. But the fourteen days were hardly routine. They were a nightmare from the start.

Camp Lejeune had become a seething cauldron of race hatred and violence.

"Upon our arrival at the base we were briefed on precautionary measures to be taken during our two-week duty," reported one of the Garden City reservists. "A ten P.M. curfew was imposed. Instructions were given to all reservists to walk in groups of no less than six at all times. We were specifically cautioned about avoiding certain enlistedmen's clubs which were labeled 'off limits' due to previous incidents."

82

Seventy-two other Marine reservists attested to the above account of the Second Battalion's arrival at Camp Lejeune. They also attested to the accuracy of reports of an incredible series of events that occurred during their two weeks at Lejeune.

The first of these occurred on their first night on base.

The last mournful notes of taps had sounded, and an uneasy stillness settled on the sultry July night. The men of the Second Battalion tried to sleep, the words of the unnerving warning upon their arrival keeping most of them awake. Then, from outside the barracks came the sounds of a large and angry mob. Outside, about sixty regular Marines from the First Battalion, 6th Marines, whose barracks were directly opposite the Second Battalion's, attempted to storm the Second's billet, threatening with clubs to inflict bodily harm on all the men inside. Only the arrival of MP's prevented a bloody clash.

A week later, a reservist was mugged on leaving the barracks. Within a short time, two sentries were attacked and severely beaten, their wallets taken by five Negro Marines. Following the assault on the two sentries, one reservist, fearful for his life, carried a knife. It was later confiscated by the MP's, who stated that it was unlawful to carry a weapon of that type on the base.

On Monday, July 14, the Second Battalion went into the field for a week of regimental-size maneuvers. A small number of reservists remained behind to perform various duties. This group was again reminded of precautions, now even more important because of the smaller number of men. The men remained in their barracks, padlocking it from the inside. The padlock prevented a forceable entry into the barracks the following night.

On succeeding days, various groups of Marines were harassed by roaming bands of Marines until the military police arrived. Numerous black Marines raised clenched fists as a sign of greeting on the base.

These growing racial tensions might not have come to the public's attention were it not for a spectacular and tragic incident on July 20. A battle between forty-four Marines, both white and black, broke out in a service club when a Negro tried to cut in on a white sailor dancing with a Negro girl. In the melee, three Marines were injured seriously enough to be hospitalized. Those injured were Corporal Edward E. Bankston, Piccayune, Mississippi; Private First Class James S. Young, Roanoke, Virginia; and Private First Class Joseph V. Baum, Jr., of Columbus, Ohio.

After the battle in the service club, about thirty Marines, mostly Negroes, engaged in a series of fights with fourteen Marines, resulting in the hospitalization of three men.

"The dance incident still has not been shown to be related to the assaults which began in the same area thirty minutes later," said a Marine Corps spokesman. "Reports are conflicting, but it happens that a white sailor was dancing with a Negro girl when a Negro Marine attempted to cut in and was refused. There was a scuffle on the dance floor, but it was stopped and the mixed couple left the club. The incident did have some racial overtone, but no evidence has been uncovered to indicate that it was a preorganized demonstration. There was a large crowd at the service club because of a farewell party for the First Battalion, 6th Marines, departing for a Mediterranean cruise on Wednesday. There have been some minor racial incidents here as in any large city, but this is the first major outbreak of violence. We have militants, both black and white."

There were indications, despite the above Marine Corps statement to the contrary, that there had been a growing number of racial incidents at Lejeune. Urgent pleas by the New York reservists to Congressman Mario Biaggi for aid told only part of the picture of racial tension at the camp. Biaggi, acting on the appeals of the New Yorkers, called for an investigation by Congress to determine if the military had been infiltrated by persons "who engage in acts of subversion." Biaggi's statements on the Lejeune racial troubles were the first public announcement that all was not well at Lejeune.

The Marine Corps, launching its own investigation of the brawls, stated that five Negroes were being held, four others were restricted, and others were being questioned. But the Corps maintained that the events of July 20 were "isolated" incidents.

Meanwhile, Corporal Bankston died of the injuries he received in the July 20 incident. He died at the Portsmouth, Virginia, naval hospital, where another of the injured men, PFC Young, contradicted the Marine Corps statement that the Lejeune riot was an isolated incident.

"There's a lot going on around there," Young said. "We've had a lot of trouble. Usually the boys would go out late at night, around ten or eleven o'clock. They'd jump one another."

This happened, according to Young, two or three times a week. He stated that the lance corporal who led his squad was threatened by a group of Negroes three nights before Young and Bankston were attacked.

Sides were being taken at Lejeune, he said, along racial lines.

Following the July 20 riot, the Marine Corps investigation led to riot charges being placed against twenty-six Marines and one sailor. All but two accused were Negroes. Two men were ultimately given dishonorable discharges and were sentenced to two years in prison.

While the race riot at Lejeune shocked much of the nation when it was reported in the press, the Marine Corps itself should not have been surprised. Nor should it have so readily concluded that the riot was an isolated incident. Three months before the incident a committee of seven officers had warned the commanding general of the 2nd Marine Division that an explosive situation of major proportions had been created and continued to be aggravated. The warning was made in a report to Major General Edwin B. Wheeler.

The report was issued by the Ad Hoc Committee on Equal Treatment and Opportunity at Camp Lejeune. It was submitted on April 22, 1969, by Colonel Louis S. Hollier. The report stated that the committee's investigation showed that despite policies "emanating from the highest echelons of Government down to and including those of the commanding general and as further expressed by organizational commanders within the division, a racial problem of considerable magnitude continues to exist and, in fact, may be expected to increase."

The committee cited two reasons for the problem. First, the Marine Corps was returning both black and white Marines to civilian society "with more deeply seated prejudices than were individually possessed upon entrance into the service." Second, conditions existed that could readily cause a minor incident not necessarily containing racial overtones to expand to a major racial confrontation. (Excerpts of the report are found in Appendix 2.)

This report never received wide distribution despite the hope of some members of the committee that drafted it that it would be circulated. One officer said the report had fallen "on deaf ears" because it was considered too open and too shocking, but Colonel Hollier said he never intended that the report be circulated. One of the ironies of the report's history is that it did not, apparently, reach General Wheeler's successor, Major General Michael P. Ryan, who took over command of the 2d Marine Division when Wheeler was assigned to duty in Vietnam. Ryan stated in an interview that he was not familiar with any report that was submitted.

Asked if he found any influence among black Marines from organizations such as the Black Panthers, Ryan said there had been some "indications" but "no tangible evidence."

Ryan, a general who entered the Marines through the reserves and rose through the ranks, is a decorated veteran of the Pacific campaign in World War II. Trim and gray at age fifty-three, he had come into the command of the 2d Marine Division at the peak of the racial brawling and tension following the July 20 service-club incident. "These assaults are irrational," he said. "Most of them are by blacks on whites. In most cases, wallets are taken. It doesn't take a study group to know that if you have tensions, and there is an assault, then there is polarization between the races."

Between January 1 and the first week of August, there had been 190 assaults. Only four of them had been a Negro assaulting another Negro. Fifty involved only whites. There were 136 involving blacks and whites. According to the provost marshall, 122 of these were blacks attacking whites while 14 were attacks of whites on blacks. The overwhelming majority—114 to 22—were on the Marine base. And the vast majority of these occurred from April through July, 1969.

This hostile environment led General Ryan to post additional sentries, with side arms and rifles and shortwave radio communication equipment, along the borderlines between the two groups of Marines. *New York Times* reporter E. W. Kenworthy described the situation: "At night, some of the sentries hide in bushes. In addition, the General has created three 'reaction forces'—25 men in one area, 15 in a second and 10 in a third—and has set a goal of three minutes for a force to reach the site of an assault or riot. The reaction forces are equipped with tear gas, arms and cameras."

This area between blacks and whites at Lejeune quickly became known as the DMZ (demilitarized zone).

Men assigned to the patrol duties were bitter. "Look at this," said one Marine veteran, "I've got seventeen years in the Corps and what do I have to do? Strap on a .45 and spend my Sunday night watching PFC's drink beer. If one of them bastards gets out of line, he's going to get it right across the teeth."

Many young enlisted men considered the camp little more than a prison. It seemed worse to young blacks. "I'll tell you what the trouble is. It's those staff NCO's always picking on you. I don't know whether it's racial. Some of them are prejudiced, some aren't," a black Marine said.

Another said, "You want to know what the trouble is? I'll tell you in one word. It's bitterness, hatred. It's in our society and it's affecting the Marines. And it's going to get worse before it gets better."

The Marines, like society, are caught in the trap of symbols. Take hair, *the* symbol of the generation gap. Young blacks insist on the right to wear "Afro" hair styles. "For the black Marine, the Afro haircut style is in," says a Marine platoon leader's pamphlet. "Such a haircut is not necessarily contrary to Marine Corps standards of appearance."

This order allowing the Afro haircut annoyed some white Marines. "I've been a skinhead all my life," said one embittered sergeant. "We all have. I don't see why these kids have to be different. They say it's their 'African heritage.' Hah!"

The use by blacks of symbols appears to be a challenge to Marines who have been taught to think of a Marine as green rather than as black, white, or yellow.

More than some commanders in our military services,

General Ryan showed not only an acute awareness of the problems of morale and discipline as they affect the Corps but also a sensitivity to the special problems of the black Marine. Several months before the Marine Corps Commandant officially recognized special black needs, Rayn issued the platoon leader's pamphlet to men under his command on "the racial situation." (See Appendix 3 for text.)

General Ryan's attempts at dealing with racial sensitivities at Lejeune were not overwhelmingly successful. Because they were in the realm of a man's attitude toward other men, they could only be as successful as individual Marines wished them to be. You cannot legislate morality, brotherhood, and understanding in the Marine Corps any more easily than these things can be legislated in civilian affairs.

The platoon leader's pamphlet, in some instances, served to alienate white Marines who were already feeling that the Corps had gone too far to placate what they considered troublemakers, agitators, and other ne'er-do-wells in the ranks. Bitterness was particularly evident among older white Marines, veterans of previous wars, who believed that the Corps's great traditions were being subverted.

"I hate to have to say this about an institution I love," said a seventeen-year veteran of the Corps, "but it's dying. There's no respect for authority any more. Men are afraid to stand up and exert their authority."

Marine NCO's say they face special problems because of black sensitivities. "You can't tell a black to clean the commode. That's 'menial labor.' But it has to be done, so you end up getting a white to do it."

Lejeune also has the added burden of its geography.

The camp is located at Jacksonville, North Carolina, in the southeastern part of the state. Outside the nearby town of Smithfield a billboard proclaims: "This is Klan country." Wallace-for-President signs abound, not leftovers from 1968, but signs boosting the segregationist Alabaman for President in 1972.

In his investigation of the Lejeune riots, Congressman Biaggi talked with police officials in Jacksonville. One of them flatly stated that black militants would overthrow the base in two to three years. He referred specifically to the influence on the base of the Black Panthers. There are no orders against black Marines belonging to the Panthers except general regulations against engaging in a conspiracy to violate laws or against belonging to an organization that is subversive. "But it would not be right to say a Marine could not have an association which has not been declared unlawful," stated General Ryan.

Individual Marines testified that blacks at Lejeune regularly gave the upraised-fist salute of the Panthers, even during the raising and lowering of the Stars and Stripes.

That off-base racial tensions find their way onto the base is inevitable, but officials and residents of communities around Lejeune say their communities are not inhospitable to blacks. Deputy Assistant Defense Secretary for Manpower, Reserves, and Civil Rights L. Howard Bennett told a news conference at Camp Lejeune that he had not heard anyone on the base say that Jacksonville was inhospitable to blacks. Bennett said he had conferred with Mayor Bruce Teachey and other city officers about Lejeune's racial problems and that the city officials were sympathetic and wanted to help. Bennett then stated the military's greatest problem was to keep civilian racial troubles from seeping onto military bases.

Of Jacksonville's contributions to Marine Corps racial problems, *Life* magazine's Paul Good wrote that Jacksonville disturbs almost all of Lejeune's Marines because it is not so much a city as it is a cash register ringing up its share of Lejeune's quarter-of-a-billion-dollar annual contribution to the state's economy.

If Jacksonville is galling to white Marines, Good observed, the city and its environs are insufferable for blacks because while there is no open, overt segregation in the bars, blacks quickly learn that they are not welcome in most.

Bennett's review of the Lejeune situation concluded with the statement that at Lejeune "there is a far greater concern among black Marines for their brothers and sisters in the civilian community who are suffering discrimination."

But blacks feel they are the victims of discrimination within the Corps itself.

To ease this feeling, the Marines took steps.

"There is no question about it, we've got a problem," said Marine Corps Commandant Leonard F. Chapman, Jr. "We thought we had eliminated discrimination in the Corps, and we are still determined to do so."

In the words of a headline writer, Chapman ordered the Marines to inject a little "soul" into the Corps. He sent a directive to all Marine commands emphasizing that leadership from officers and NCO's was needed to help the Corps deal with its racial problems. Certain gestures toward black sensitivities were permitted, including the modified Afro haircut. Grievances when expressed were to be quickly investigated. (The text of the Commandant's directive is contained in Appendix 4.)

The Commandant's order to his Marines was prompted not only by the Lejeune difficulties. On August 10, 1969, fighting between Negroes and whites resulted in injuries to sixteen Marines at Kaneohe Marine Corps Air Station in Hawaii. "Preliminary investigation disclosed that racial overtones were involved," said a Corps spokesman. A Marine who was afraid to give newsmen his name stated that relations between the races had been strained for several months at Kaneohe, headquarters for the First Marine Brigade. The Honolulu *Star Bulletin* reported that troubles began after about fifty Negroes gave the black-power clenched-fist salute when the colors were lowered on the base. Some Marines said they could not feel safe on the base unless they slept with their bayonets at the ready.

A lance corporal who feared reprisal and who asked not to have his name published said he had observed "increasing racial problems" at the Marine Corps Air Station, El Toro, Santa Ana, California. He stated, "The common symbol of the 'Black Power' movement can be seen anywhere at any time on base—the closed fist raised in the air." He cited cases of attacks on white Marines by blacks in the chow line, after lights-out in the barracks, and in other situations. "This situation exists," he said, "on the air base where the President of the United States lands to go by 'chopper' to his San Clemente home."

In reply to increasing charges that organized black militant groups are active in the Marine Corps, a Navy Department officer stated that "there is no evidence of an organized movement by minority groups in the Navy," of which the Marine Corps is part.

Inevitably, these reports of racial rioting on Marine bases aroused the interest of the House Armed Services Committee, whose chairman is L. Mendel Rivers, Democrat of South Carolina. Rivers announced on August 1, 1969, that his committee would look into "acts of militancy . . . brawls and fights" at Lejeune and other military posts. Rivers appointed Representative William J. Randall, Democrat of Missouri, to head a special subcommittee and directed him to hold hearings both in Washington and at the installations where disruptions had taken place.

Rivers acted after Representative Biaggi had called publicly for such an investigation and after Biaggi had made an investigation of his own, a fact that did not sit well with the chairman of the Armed Services Committee of the House. On learning of Rivers' intention to probe the racial problems of the military, Biaggi rose on the floor of the House on August 5, saying, "The recognition of the problem by the Armed Services Committee and its desire to try to do something about it is surely a step in the right direction." But, Biaggi wondered, what would be the results of the Armed Services Committee probe? "There are those who have told me that the fact that the Armed Services Committee showed no visible awareness of the problem until I called attention to it is, perhaps, the best evidence of that committee's burdens with so many other matters. It is hard to argue against logic of that sort."

Biaggi preferred an investigation by a committee other than Armed Services. He offered a resolution for the creation of a select committee composed of seven members of the House for the purpose of inquiring into all aspects of crime and disorder on American military installations. The suggestion was greeted coolly, at best, by Rivers and his committee.

There developed between Biaggi and the Rivers committee an open hostility growing out of Rivers' belief that the military is his private domain and Biaggi's contention that, at best, Rivers' handling of military matters was prejudiced in favor of the military. Few commentators and analysts of the Washington scene made note of the dispute between the freshman Bronx Democrat and the senior South Carolina Democrat, but it is a development that may be an indication of an historic break with the traditions of Congress that have placed enormous power in the hands of men of great seniority on influential committees. (The full Biaggi-Rivers squabble and the powerful House Committee on Armed Services are discussed in detail later.)

Rising on the floor of the House after hearing Biaggi's August 5 speech, Representative Randall stated that "it is more properly the jurisdiction of the Committee on

Armed Services to look into military problems rather than a select committee."

Randall stated that Chairman Rivers had been aware of the troubles at Marine bases because of a report from the Commandant and that Rivers had been preparing to launch an investigation into the matter even before Biaggi was publicly suggesting a probe.

Despite Randall's assertions, there was no indication from the House Armed Services Committee of its intention to investigate racial rioting and other racial problems on Marine bases. Not, in fact, until after Biaggi's suggestion of a special investigating committee did the Armed Services Committee act. Yet in its report on the investigation of the Lejeune riot the Armed Services Committee offered ample evidence that a serious racial crisis had been brewing in the Corps. The only conclusion to be drawn is that the House Armed Services Committee would not have investigated racial problems if there had not been a spectacular incident such as the one of July 20.

Under the chairmanship of William J. Randall, the Special Subcommittee to Probe Disturbances on Military Bases began work. Its members included G. Elliott Hagan, Georgia; Robert H. Mollohan, West Virginia; W. C. (Dan) Daniel, Virginia; Alexander Pirnie, New York; Donald C. Clancy, Ohio; and John E. Hunt, New Jersey. Their counsel was William H. Hogan, Jr. The report of these men was based on hearings at Camp Lejeune and in Washington, covering some 1,250 pages of testimony and documents.

The report reviewed the history of attempts at racial integration in the armed services and at Lejeune prior to the July 20 riot. "There is no doubt that this tragic event had racial overtones," the report stated, rejecting the contention that it was an isolated incident. The report's findings state:

1. The racial problem existing at Camp Lejeune is a reflection of the nation's racial problem.

2. The average young black Marine has racial pride, drive for identity, and sensitivity to discrimination that is characteristic of the young black in the United States.

3. The Marine Corps and the other services have led the way and made substantial progress in integration of the races since 1948.

4. Racial disturbances and misunderstandings at Camp Lejeune can be attributed in large measure to lack of effective communication at the junior levels of command as well as vertically between the young Marine and his commander.

5. A shortage of mature leadership attributed in large measure to rapid buildup and turnover at the NCO and junior officer levels at Camp Lejeune has aggravated the racial problem.

6. There was a deterioration in discipline at Camp Lejeune.

7. The instances of permissiveness appearing at the junior levels of command are damaging to discipline but unfortunately mirror the society in which these young men live.

8. The security procedures at Camp Lejeune on the evening of July 20 were insufficient, despite some warning of impending trouble.

9. Improved security measures are necessary at the ammunition storage areas and armories, as well as improved lighting in populated areas throughout the Camp Lejeune complex.

10. The fatality which occurred did not result from any misconduct on the part of the victim.

The report concluded: "The serious racial disturbance at Camp Lejeune on July 20 did not result from any specific provocation, but was generated by a few militant blacks who fanned the flames of racism, misconceptions, suspicions and frustrations."

The subcommittee recommended a program to foster communications between the races, including discussion

groups and full utilization of existing procedures for Marines to express their gripes to their commanders. It also
stated, "The militants compose only a small minority of
[the Marines] . . . and such organizations as the Black Panthers have no foothold on our military bases although the
danger of their influence is very real and must be carefully watched."

Communications and leadership, the subcommittee said,
were the only way to solve racial troubles in the armed
services. "The subcommittee is of the opinion that this
investigation has identified root causes of the race problems at Camp Lejeune which are also typical of those of
any military base," the report states. "The shortcomings and
differences have been earmarked and with the basic leadership guidance which the Commandant of the Marine
Corps assured us is most adequate, we expect that the problems will be attacked as a matter of urgency and that the
possibility of a repetition of the tragic events of July 20
will be materially lessened."

With those words, the House Armed Services Committee dismissed the Lejeune race riot and the other alarming racial troubles plaguing other military installations.

The report appears simplistic and dangerous, not least
of all because it indicates that the House Armed Services
Committee considers that it can wash its hands of the matter by simply telling the Marines that they have a problem
and that the committee feels the utmost confidence in the
Marines to solve it. It is rather like a physician telling a
patient that he has an illness but that the doctor has the
utmost confidence that, now knowing about the illness, the
patient will be able to treat it successfully himself. And
to dismiss the racial troubles of the armed services as
"a reflection of the nation's racial problem" is a whitewash.
This desire to leave the problem solely with the military
unfortunately extends into the civilian administration of
the Department of Defense. On February 3, 1970, Secretary

of Defense Melvin R. Laird stated, "It is a fact . . . that the armed forces have a race problem because our nation has a race problem." He ordered each service to "examine in depth its own communications to judge whether or not it promotes better understanding between the races."

These are admirable intentions expressed by the top civilians in our armed services. They are as lofty in intent as the directives handed down by the Marine Corps Commandant and General Ryan, several months before Secretary Laird's general order. They recognize the need to deal with the race problem in the armed services, but one wonders if a round-table discussion of problems will be of any value to the Marine NCO who needs someone to clean the latrine, fears that to ask a black Marine to do it will be interpreted as a racial slur, and therefore turns to a white Marine for the chore, only to find that the white Marine thereafter feels that *he* has been the victim of racial discrimination. The loftiest goals of human brotherhood translate with great difficulty into a military work situation. In the Marines, where a large number of the men involved in these situations are not well educated, the subtleties of racial harmony as envisioned by the top brass may be hard to grasp.

The Afro haircut is a case in point. Designed to give black Marines a feeling of identity, the Afro haircut became for many white Marines a symbol of reverse discrimination. The blacks were being made exceptions in a Corps that traditionally did not allow exceptions. There has been some misunderstanding, however, about just what the order allowing an Afro haircut really stated. There are regulations regarding the Afro. "Obviously it can't be a bushy Afro such as you'd find on an actor or someone like that," a Marine officer pointed out. "It must be neatly trimmed and within the three-inch regulation." Once the regulation allowing the Afro style was issued, the wearing of it was not as widespread as expected. But there was resentment from whites on the basis of their recognition that one Marine was allowed something another was not. The Afro haircut was never, and is not now, allowed in boot camp. There, all haircuts are the same—bald.

The difficulties that the Marines encountered over the Afro haircut arose from a breakdown in communication. It took a while before everyone learned that what was being permitted was a *modified* Afro. There was increased racial tension as a result. In retrospect, it may be that allowing the Afro haircut was a mistake and that the Marines should have not permitted exceptions, no matter how much pressure there was from black militants.

Not all pressure comes from blacks. Waldo Lyon made these observations about the pressures applied to the Corps in matters of race and about his opinion of the Corps's performance on racial matters:

> The Marine Corps has found it expeditious to avoid offending the white power-structure in towns near Parris Island. When several black enlisted Marines were promoted to officer status in the summer of 1966, it was remarkable to note how swiftly their orders for Vietnam arrived. A less coincidental event found the officers' golf group instituting personalized invitations to officers to ensure that no black Navy or Marine Corps officer took part in a golf match with a local civilian country club. It was hardly surprising that no official Marine Corps representative attended the local biracial ecumenical memorial service for Dr. Martin Luther King, Jr.
>
> In recruit training, on the other hand, there is no distinction between recruits as to race or creed. The disadvantaged and the dropout are treated no worse than other recruits. Although mass punishment is theoretically forbidden, most platoons learn the hard fact that a chain is no stronger than its weakest link. There is true brotherhood among recruits at Parris Island as in Vietnam.
>
> There are positive lessons to be gained from this

survey of Marine Corps training practices. The military has been fairly successful, at least on the enlisted level, in enforcing integration, particularly in Vietnam. The Negro reenlistment rate has been consistently higher. There has been progress made toward desegregating civilian housing, even in the South.

No one is more aware of the Marines' racial problems than Colonel Raymond Henri, head of the Equal Opportunity Branch of Marine Headquarters in Washington. "Basically, the main need is the exercising of good leadership," he says, but he finds that the Vietnam war has created special problems in the area of leadership. "This is a very peculiar war. One of the problems is that most of the young officers have no experience with their troops except in battle, because of the speed with which they are trained and sent overseas. When they come back into a barracks situation they run into trouble, because they have not developed a father-son relationship between an officer and an enlisted man. They've had no time for it."

As for the black Marine, Henri thinks he's done fairly well in the Corps. He states that the proportion of blacks in the Corps is about equal to their proportion in the general population, while the number of blacks in the higher pay grades in Marine enlisted ranks is higher than the proportion of better-paid blacks in civilian employment. Commenting on both the Commandant's and the Defense Secretary's urging of better communications, Colonel Henri says that the Marines have a good record. "These have been created and the round-table discussions are taking place in every Marine Corps unit independently."

"It's on liberty that the problems arise," he says.

He spoke with some bitterness about the attitude of some civilians toward men in uniform. "The uniform is not popular in this war," he observed. "A man comes home in uniform and he's immediately surrounded by his old friends saying, 'You dumb son of a bitch, what are you doing fighting Vietnamese?' There was a time when you'd be proud to go home in uniform, the community would have been proud to welcome you home. No more. This is not a popular war, and that makes a big difference."

What are the solutions to these problems?

Colonel Henri thinks it's a matter of "seeing to it that all Marines are properly sensitized, that the white Marine understands the problems of black Marines and that blacks understand whites."

The Marine Corps itself is officially making note of the special problems of blacks in its ranks by devising testing programs that are not ethnically oriented. Some of the tests now given are meaningless to blacks who take them. They don't understand the language and score poorly. To overcome this problem, the Marines have instituted studies on revising their examinations so that they will not reflect, as they now do, the white society on which they are based. These exams are presently being developed and tested and will come into general use throughout the Marine Corps.

The Corps has been sensitive to criticism based on statistics that show black Marines had a higher casualty rate in Vietnam than white Marines. Charges were made that this was due to the Corps's inherent racism. But the explanation is far less sinister, although, as the Corps recognizes, not exactly satisfactory. "The reason for higher black casualties," explains Colonel Henri, "is that the black boot, with his comparative lack of education and ability to pass tests, does not qualify for the military occupational specialties that are open to those qualified. So most blacks come out with only the basic fighting skills."

The Corps hopes that its ethnic testing program will alleviate this form of discrimination and that blacks entering the Corps will be able to move into noncombat military occupations with as much ease as whites. This should lower the number of blacks in the basic infantryman category and reduce the disproportionate casualty rate.

In response to criticism that it does not permit blacks to become officers, the Corps replies with figures that showed in early 1970 a total of 296 black officers in the Corps out of a total black Marine strength of 23,109, or better than 11 per cent. Criticism charging the Corps with discrimination against blacks as officers is unfounded. The Corps does not now have a black general and probably will not have one before 1980, but this is due to the natural course of promotion and not to racial discrimination.

The Marines believe their racial problems stem from two causes—white prejudice and black awakening. "Naturally, you're going to have tensions," observed Colonel Henri, "but if we seek for an open communication between the two of them, I think we'll be all right."

Communication is the key, of course, but it seems reasonable that the communication flow must be begun in a dramatic and meaningful way. What is needed is a thorough examination of the racial dilemma by persons not connected with the established upper echelons of government, civilian and military. As admirable as the Defense Department's investigations of its racial problems may be, it is impossible for an organization to be completely objective while investigating itself. The House Committee on Armed Services' special investigation of the racial problems on military installations was equally limited in its objectivity because the Armed Services Committee is simply too close to the military to be objective about it.

Who, then, should take a look at race relations in our armed services? Generals? Congressmen? A select committee of citizens chosen by the President? Civil-rights leaders? Probably not.

No one knows better the day-to-day problems of getting along with the guy in the next bunk or the nearest foxhole than the enlisted man.

What seems to be a reasonable recommendation to us is a committee of men from the armed services, none above the rank of sergeant but including all enlisted grades, from all the services. Their chairman might be a justice of the United States Supreme Court who would aid and advise these men in the choice of counsel, investigators, and staff. The panel would be appointed by the President of the United States and would have all the powers of subpoena that any Presidential commission would have. The panel would be racially balanced and, as nearly as possible, reflective of the sort of men who serve in our armed services—draftees, enlisted men, career noncoms, combat veterans, noncombatants. The panel would report directly to the President of the United States with its findings of causes of racial troubles and would make recommendations.

The chances for the establishment of such a panel are probably not very good. There would be strong resistance from the vested interests, not only in the armed services and the Congress, but among civilian civil rights groups, veterans organizations, and other political bodies.

Professional social scientists will ask what qualifications this panel of GI's would have for looking into the complex and sophisticated problems of human relations. Powerful Congressmen will howl at the thought that someone other than a member of Congress has the power to investigate an arm of the government. Racists on both sides will claim that not enough of this race or that one is on the panel.

But the commanding reason *for* such a GI panel to probe racial problems in the armed services is simply that these are the men who are most directly involved, who have the most to lose by continued racial stresses, and who have the most to gain from constructive and imaginative solutions.

CHAPTER EIGHT

WHITEWASH

*A serviceman may write, call, or visit
my district or Washington office.*
                                    A member of Congress

"Personnel availing themselves of the right to correspond
with individual Members of Congress . . . may do so without fear of prejudice to their interests," say the Marines.

These may be encouraging words to a Marine who feels
that he has no one to whom to turn for help, but in fact
there is likely to be disappointment and frustration rather
than aid and comfort awaiting the Marine who jots down
an urgent appeal to his Congressman, because the Congressman in virtually every instance will simply refer the
case back to the Marines.

Representative James H. Scheuer, of New York, outlined
for the authors the procedures generally followed by members of Congress when they are asked for assistance by
members of the armed forces:

1. A request for congressional intervention must be made
by the serviceman himself, except in one instance (a
health and welfare check, which may be requested by someone else).

2. Inquiries into a problem are made with the military *only after* the serviceman has made his request with the military and submitted any necessary supporting documents.

3. Once the requisite steps have been taken, a Congressman can make an inquiry with the military to support a case and to show interest. *The military will consider this along with all other evidence, and then make its own decision.*

"A serviceman may write, call, or visit my district or Washington office," explained Representative Scheuer. "Congressional inquiries are made from my Washington office through the use of the military liaison on Capitol Hill or in the Pentagon."

In 1969, 110 military cases were handled in this manner by Representative Scheuer. Seventeen of these involved Marines. The most frequent Marine Corps requests for help include humanitarian transfers, hardship discharges, medical attention, military discipline, and health and welfare.

"As one might expect," wrote Scheuer, "many of the problems overlap. For example, if a Marine is confined to military jail because of insubordination and an AWOL charge, he may feel that he received a 'bad deal' because racial discrimination was involved from his point of view. To further complicate matters, he might have gone AWOL because he felt that a sick mother needed him, and the Marine Corps had decided not to approve his hardship discharge."

Scheuer also stated, "Many Marines, as well as other servicemen, have voluntarily joined the armed forces and find later it is not at all what they expected."

Congressmen like Scheuer try to help the men who write to them, but in most cases the serviceman seeking aid is due for disappointment, because, in fact, there is little that the individual member of Congress can do forcefully to assist a man. In effect, all he can do is let the military know he is aware of a man's case. Except for one segment of the Capitol Hill membership, the military will not likely be impressed by inquiries from Congressmen.

The only members of Congress who have any power at the Pentagon are the members of the Armed Services Committees of the Senate and House. But even with these two groups, the military's real concern is limited.

Of the two committees, it is the one in the House that really matters, and that committee is jealous of its power and influence in the Pentagon.

When Representative Biaggi suggested, as a result of his investigations of problems at Camp Lejeune and Parris Island, that there be a thorough investigation of the conditions in the military, Biaggi said that the probe should be made by a select committee of the House rather than by the House Committee on Armed Services. The chairman of that committee was distressed because Biaggi had taken it upon himself to deal with a military matter without consulting him. Lucius Mendel Rivers is a prideful man who regards matters military as his exclusive domain on Capitol Hill.

Rivers was furious about Biaggi's resolution proposing the select committee to investigate the military and responded to the intrusion on his prerogatives by promptly announcing that the Armed Services Committee would investigate the reports of disorders on military bases. Rivers referred to them as "acts of militancy . . . brawls and fights." He appointed Representative William J. Randall as chairman of a special subcommittee.

Biaggi, speaking on the floor, observed, "I would be less than truthful . . . if I did not say that I would prefer the formation of a permanent select committee that would deal solely with this most important investigation and not be burdened with other responsibilities."

As Biaggi spoke, Randall was sitting in the visitors' gallery above the floor, talking with some constituents from his home state of Missouri. He hushed that conversation immediately and listened intently to Biaggi.

"There are those who have told me that the fact that the Armed Services Committee showed no visible awareness of the problem until I called attention to it is, perhaps, the best evidence of that committee's burdens with so many other matters. It is hard to argue against logic of that sort. We must wait and see and hope for the best," Biaggi said.

Representative Randall hurriedly left the gallery and went to the floor, asking to be heard.

William J. Randall, a Democrat, born in Independence, Missouri, on July 16, 1909, was first elected to Congress in 1959 to fill an unexpired term. He is a veteran of World War II, a judge, and high on the seniority list of the Armed Services Committee.

"Mr. Speaker," Randall stated in reply to Biaggi, "I want to assure the gentleman from New York that it is the intention of the chairman of our full committee as well as the chairman he named of the subcommittee to conduct a very thorough investigation. We plan to take whatever time is needed and to go wherever necessary to get the facts and then evaluate them.

"I submit that it is more properly the jurisdiction of the Committee on Armed Services to look into military problems rather than a select committee."

The opening rounds had been fired in a skirmish between the freshman New Yorker, Biaggi, and the established hierarchy of the House Armed Services Committee, chaired by Rivers. While these were only the opening shots, they are significant because they focus attention on the power that rests within the Armed Services Committee of the House and show how staunchly that power is defended against all usurpers by Chairman Rivers.

The chairman had made up his mind to put the freshman New Yorker in his place.

"In your speech on the floor yesterday," Rivers wrote to Biaggi, "I note that you offered to provide the Armed Services Committee with your records and reports concerning disturbances on military bases.

"This is a very generous offer of yours, and I take this opportunity to request that you make these records and reports available. . . ."

Randall informed Biaggi that he would like him to appear before the special subcommittee on August 12. Biaggi noted that the subcommittee wasn't giving him much time to organize a presentation. He asked for and got an extension of the date for his testimony.

In the meantime, a newspaper column by Jack Anderson appeared, which quoted Rivers as saying to an unnamed colonel, "We have to get that boy [Biaggi] on our team."

Anderson stated that Rivers was only mildly provoked when Biaggi went to Lejeune to conduct his own investigation of the July 20 riot, but that Rivers turned white with inner rage when Biaggi suggested the select committee to investigate disorders and lawlessness on military bases. Anderson stated that "Rivers quietly returned to his office and telephoned all committee chairmen to notify them that Biaggi has 'broken with tradition' " in challenging the Armed Services Committee's ability to handle the investigations.

"On Capitol Hill, where seniority reigns serene, an offense against tradition and the seniority system is akin to breaking the First Commandment. Hereafter, Biaggi will be lucky if he's permitted to investigate the House beauty shop," wrote Anderson.

Biaggi regarded the Anderson column as a phony story deliberately planted to get Biaggi back into line. "Rivers was putting out a feeler to determine whether Biaggi was with him or against him," said Dom Frasca, a Biaggi aide. "Biaggi did not take the bait."

On September 16 Biaggi appeared before the Randall subcommittee in Room 2216 of the massive Rayburn Building on Capitol Hill. He summarized his knowledge of the racial incidents at Camp Lejeune, brutality and maltreatment of recruits at Parris Island, and other findings unearthed by his personal investigations.

"In my opinion," said Biaggi, "the best evidence of the seriousness of the problem can be found on military bases where commanding officers have had to increase the policing of ammunition dumps. The fact that this had to be done seems to pose a question of national security."

Stating that he had heard ranking military officers juggle facts and statistics to play down the problem, Biaggi noted that he had read an article in which subcommittee Chairman Randall was quoted as saying that racial disturbances on military bases were "much fewer" than generally believed.

"The common practice seems to be to describe every outbreak of violence as an 'isolated incident.' I do not understand this practice. I believe it to be foolish and dangerous," Biaggi stated. He went on to testify:

> Speak to the enlisted men and the noncommissioned officers on any of the bases that I have mentioned in my testimony today and see if they tell you that racial strife, assaults, and general disorders on their bases are isolated incidents. If anything, we cut further into the demoralization of our troops when we try to sweep the problem under the rug.
>
> Above all, we must remember that American boys are not only dying on foreign soil, but their lives are also being jeopardized presently right within the confines of some of our own military installations.

It was claimed in one syndicated column recently that I, as a freshman member of this Congress, violated tradition by "raising a howl about black Marines beating up white Marines." I can only say that the record is clear on that score. I have spent my entire adult life fighting bigotry of every kind. As for tradition, I recognize it and respect it—but I would be less than truthful if I did not say that I give priority to serving my constituents and our nation. If the pursuit of that purpose violates tradition in the opinion of some, then so be it.

Biaggi again urged the establishment of a select committee to look into the problems on our military bases.

The Randall subcommittee listened politely, with no indication that the proposal for the special investigating committee would be given serious consideration.

A few Members of the House, however, were rallying to the project. One of them, Allard J. Lowenstein, of New York, said:

We should undertake this investigation as soon as possible, and the military should welcome it. Servicemen of all races, of all ranks, as well as Americans committed to upholding the Constitution of this country, should insist that we stop abdicating this function that can be undertaken properly only by the Congress, in the wake of the burgeoning doubts about so many aspects of military justice and discipline. There have been too many peculiar episodes, from the Presidio to Camp Lejeune, that have left the public troubled and mystified—troubled about conditions in stockades, about the fairness of military justice, about the protection of servicemen from violence, at least while they are on bases in this country. It would be in everybody's interest to have these problems investigated with energy and impartiality so what is cloudy can be cleared up, so what is wrong can be righted.

The investigation of "energy and impartiality" that Representative Lowenstein hoped for was not forthcoming from the House Armed Services Committee, which buried the Biaggi resolution.

Biaggi charged that "the House Armed Services Committee has claimed it would investigate some of the more serious military problems—but to date I have seen no real evidence of a genuine investigation. In fact, indications have led me to believe that the committee is determined to play down the problems and ultimately disregard them."

How could a member of Congress reach such a conclusion about a committee of the House? Sadly, Biaggi's suspicions that the House Armed Services Committee would do little more than sweep the military's problems under the rug were based on the record of the committee and its chairman, Lucius Mendel Rivers. Biaggi's conclusions were made on the basis of the committee's history, which is replete with charges by its critics that it is little more than an arm of the Pentagon and as much a part of the so-called military-industrial complex as any defense contractor or four-star general. That the military remains largely sacrosanct and secure is due in no small measure to the friendly atmosphere that is generated toward the armed services by the House Armed Services Committee.

Established with forty members, the Armed Services Committee is charged by the House to look into matters dealing with (1) the common defense generally, (2) the Department of Defense generally, including the Departments of the Army, Navy, and Air Force generally, (3) ammunition depots, forts, arsenals, and Army, Navy, and Air Force reservations and establishments, (4) conservation, development, and use of Naval petroleum and oil-shale reserves, (5) pay, promotion, retirement, and other benefits and privileges of members of the armed forces, (6) scientific research and development in support of the armed services, (7) selective services, (8) size and composition of the Army, Navy, and Air Force, (9) soldiers' and sailors' homes, and (10) strategic and critical materials necessary for the common defense.

This mandate from the House puts supervision of the entire military-industrial complex into the hands of the committee and makes it responsible for the supervision of the massive American defense budget. There is no more powerful committee in the Congress. No single group of Congressmen has so much to say about the spending of taxpayers' dollars. No one committee has so much control over the destiny of the American military machinery.

All of that power is at the disposal of one man, the committee chairman, L. Mendel Rivers. Born in Berkeley County, South Carolina, on September 5, 1905, Rivers was educated in public schools, the College of Charleston, and the University of South Carolina. He was admitted to the South Carolina bar in 1932, served in the state legislature, and was elected to Congress on November 5, 1940. He has served there ever since. He holds honorary memberships in the Fleet Reserve Association, National Guard Association, and the Air Force Sergeants Association.

In a Drew Pearson column written by Jack Anderson, it was said of the Armed Services Committee chairman:

> Rivers has attained his eminence in military affairs, of course, because of his ability to outlive men of more talent and because of his foresight in being born in an area that still treasures the one-party system. This has given him the seniority that has elevated him, escalator fashion, to the chairmanship of the Armed Services Committee and given him sway over the nation's 3.5 million servicemen.
>
> He runs his committee with pomposity and treats his committee members like lackeys and lieutenants.

Rivers bore no great love for Pearson and Anderson, noting in a letter to a man in Staten Island, New York, that had he the power to control what a columnist says about any member of Congress, "knowing my difficulties with a certain columnist now deceased, I certainly would have attempted to exercise control over what I consider to be libelous statements."

But Rivers *does* have power to control members of Congress. One Congressional aide stated:

> Why don't other members of Congress get up in arms about this? Why don't they fight for the cause of servicemen to improve their lot? The stories prevalent in Washington give the answer. When Mendel Rivers wants your vote, he'll count the military installations in your state. He'll call you over to the office and say, "Now look, you've got two installations in your state and you need this. You've got so many civilian employees. Are we going to get together?" If there is a plan to put a military installation somewhere, it's pretty much decided on the way the House Armed Services Committee wants it to go. So you have certain members of Congress who will stand on their heads for Mendel Rivers.

The Pentagon, too, will do headstands. They know that Chairman Rivers is a friend. In the words of *Life* magazine, Rivers "appears inordinately enamored of the military." He seems to like the military personally, but he likes it, too, because it has proved to be a boon to his home state. The area around Charleston, South Carolina, has become festooned with military installations, including an Air Force base, a Polaris missile submarine training base, an Army depot, a Naval base, the Parris Island Marine Corps Training Depot, a Marine air station, a Coast Guard station, and the headquarters of the Sixth Naval District. Rivers boasts that he brought 90 per cent of those installations into the state.

A constituent put it more colorfully to a reporter. "Mendel's got a sweet finger," he said. There is no question that

Mendel Rivers personally converted sleepy, Southern, lovely South Carolina into one of the most heavily fortified areas of the world. Rivers himself is from Gumville, South Carolina, although he now has a house in Charleston.

In Washington, Rivers lives inconspicuously in a red-brick house in McLean, Virginia. But his real home is on Capitol Hill, with his committee. "My committee gets along just fine," he says. He regards only five or six of the forty members as troublesome, but he has no worries about keeping them in line. He has been known to stand up indignantly on the floor of the House to remind a rebellious Congressman of recent courtesies extended to his district, meaning a defense contract of some kind. The sweet finger can turn sour quickly.

Rivers runs the committee on Armed Services with an iron hand and with the help of two other men. One is the ranking Republican on the committee, Leslie Arends of Illinois. Should the Republicans gain control of the House, Arends would become the chairman of the Armed Services Committee. The other man to whom Rivers turns for considerable aid in doing the committee's business is its chief of staff and counsel, John R. Blandford, a fifty-three-year old major general in the United States Marine Corps Reserves. Blandford was born in Buffalo, New York, is a graduate of the Yale Law School, and is a Phi Beta Kappa. Entering active duty in the Marines in 1941 as a second lieutenant, he rose to the rank of major by war's end and then further upward in the reserves to his present rank, the promotion to major general having been made last year.

Americans may rightly wonder about the propriety of a Marine Reserve general serving as the chief counsel for the House Committee whose job it is to watchdog the Pentagon.

A member of the Armed Services Committee summed

up the Rivers-Blandford team with the lament that the committee can hold hearings and take testimony for weeks only to find that Rivers and General Blandford draw up the bill themselves.

Both Rivers and Blandford are well-known at the Pentagon. Both are feared and respected for the power they wield over military programs and spending.

Yet throughout his years as chairman of the Armed Services Committee, Rivers has been a true friend of the military. In hearings on a military construction bill of the Ninety-First Congress, Rivers said to Rear Admiral A. C. Hudson, "We need all the friends we can get on this floor [of the House]. If you read the paper, the military complex isn't doing so well on the floor. Of course, I think we can win."

Nor is Rivers alone on the committee in his high regard for the military establishment. Representative Durward G. Hall of Missouri told Marine General William C. Chip, assistant quartermaster general of the Marine Corps, "Don't take all the austerity out of the Marine Corps. Some of them are pretty proud about the fact that they can make do, and we don't cotton necessarily to all this modern sophisticated socialization of brigs and everything else, in any of the services, and particularly in the Marine Corps that is always the firstest with the mostest."

Another member of the Armed Services Committee has extremely close ties with the military. New York Republican Alexander Pirnie was personally chosen by former Selective Service Director Louis Hershey to draw the lots in the 1969 draft lottery selection, not only because Pirnie and Hershey were personal friends but because Pirnie was a proven friend of the military.

But the really true friend is Mr. Rivers, chairman of the Armed Services Committee, a committee which the Savannah *Morning News* says "is not a post for 'doves.' "

The newspaper, on February 6, 1970, let it be known that it was backing Rivers for reelection in the 1970 elections, Rivers's sixteenth term if elected, which was a consummation never in doubt.

"Is there anything more certain than death and taxes?" asked the South Carolina newspaper. "Yes," it answered, "reelection for Rep. L. Mendel Rivers."

In its editorial, the Savannah *Morning News* caught the very essence of the phenomenon that is Mendel Rivers:

> While most politicians would rather be right AND President, Rep. Rivers would rather be Chairman of House Armed Services Committee—a post exposed more recently to flak from Congressional Liberals, but one whose citadel is more than ably manned.
>
> Some folks might refer to Mr. Rivers' district as "Pentagon South," but any constituency expects the same of its own Congressman; the trouble is, only a handful can really deliver. And while Rep. Rivers is looking out for the homefolks, he's also doing a mighty fine job for the nation. That chairmanship is not a post for "doves," any more than the agriculture committee is a job for a general. It takes a strong hand, and it takes an outlook unwilling to dismantle our military capability.
>
> That a closer look is needed at some of those military spending programs is a legitimate expectation. But at the same time, Rep. Rivers keeps us mindful that a strong military is acutely essential to having ANY programs—defensive or domestic.

Were the statements of the Savannah newspaper the only aspects of Rivers' career that we must be aware of, Chairman Rivers would probably deserve all the praise the newspaper heaps upon him. But Chairman Rivers is, by most other observations, much too friendly with the Pentagon.

The House Armed Services Committee under Rivers has usually served to protect the Defense Department, to cover up its errors, and to shield it from criticism. No one steps forward more readily to defend the Defense Department against the slings and arrows of its enemies than Rivers. The Pentagon reciprocates by giving Rivers all the deference and respect he feels he deserves. Yet it is this committee that has the responsibility of overseeing the Pentagon, of studying its needs, looking at its budget, finding its weaknesses and shortcomings.

There is, of course, a Senate Committee on Armed Services, but because the House initiates money bills, the real power lies with Rivers, not the Senate. Rivers often takes a condescending tone toward the Senate body, warning the Pentagon that its friends are not in "the other body."

Any challenge by any members of the House to Rivers and his domination of his committee is regarded by Rivers as an affront to the venerated seniority system of the Congress, a system whereby length of service in the Congress determines positions on committees and, therefore, one's power. Rivers never loses battles against upstarts who try to change the seniority system, a fact that led one of the younger Congressmen to lament that the seniority system covers everything on Capitol Hill "except the use of the public restrooms. There, at least, we have equal rights."

Rivers knows that as a Congressman moves higher in seniority he will come to defend the system. In the meantime, a call to remind the younger member about this naval station or that defense contract usually carries the day.

Little wonder, then, that the Armed Service Committee's investigation of military disorders held little promise for those concerned about the morale and safety of men involved in them. From the start, the Randall subcommittee seemed bent on obscuring the facts about racial troubles in the armed services. A Washington columnist charged that the investigators were obligingly closing doors instead of opening them. When the subcommittee looked into allegations of maltreatment in the stockade at Fort Dix, New Jersey, the Congressmen seemed eager to play down accounts of maltreatment, possibly because they came from political radicals who had incited a riot.

Too often such Congressional visits to military installations are nothing but junkets. "You see, they can't do enough for visiting Congressmen," said Dom Frasca. "They do a snow job. They wine you, dine you—in fact, we heard of cases where Congressmen have gone down there [to Parris Island], drank excessively, and even if they wanted broads —you go to the general's place and get some underling there to get you whatever you want. It is just unbelievable. You can't make any progress . . . because that House Armed Services Committee is so damned powerful."

The United States Marine Corps has been especially favored by the committee, as General Blandford, the committee counsel, stated in a hearing on February 3, 1969. He noted that "the Marine Corps has been well taken care of by this committee and by the Congress over the years."

The Marines have taken care of Blandford, too. A brigadier general in the reserves when he made the above statement, he has recently been promoted to major general.

To the authors, General Blandford wrote, "For many years this committee has been alert to the need for maintaining the Marine Corps as a distinct and permanent arm of our organization for national security . . . . I have particular reference to the unique legal status of the Commandant in the Joint Chiefs of Staff."

Blandford refers to sections of the National Security Act of 1947, as amended, which elevates the Commandant of the Marine Corps to a coequal level with the other members of the Joint Chiefs of Staff, the principal military advisers to the President, the National Security Council, and the Secretary of Defense, when the Joint Chiefs have under consideration a matter concerning the Marine Corps. This same act also protects the Marine Corps from being eliminated as a section of our armed services, a proposal which has been made in the past with considerable seriousness by some.

"We have not had that problem for about fifteen or sixteen years," boasted General Blandford, "and much is due to this committee that did many things such as put the Commandant of the Marine Corps on the Joint Chiefs of Staff."

The House Armed Services Committee also showed considerable interest in a proposal to provide the grade of general for the Assistant Commandant of the Marine Corps. This proposal was advanced by the Corps itself, which felt that the Assistant Commandant was being outranked by officers in the military services of foreign countries, though in fact they were equals. The Marines also claimed that other branches of the American armed services had two equivalent four-star generals and that the Corps was entitled to the same. To bring such a matter to the attention of the Congress, the Marine Corps maintains what is, in effect, a lobbyist on Capitol Hill.

Lieutenant Colonel Joel Bonner, a redheaded, young-looking man, is officially listed as a Congressional liaison man, and although he becomes involved in lobbying on behalf of the Corps in matters such as the added star for the shoulder of the Assistant Commandant, he also deals with the Congress when individual Marines or their families contact Congressmen with complaints or problems. "About 1 per cent of all Marines write or talk to their Congressmen, either directly or through relatives," Colonel Bonner explained. "There are 300,000 men in the Marine Corps, and 3,000 of these figure they can get help from their Congressmen. Most of these complaints go directly to the House Armed Services Committee's Chairman, Mendel Rivers."

But Bonner's chief concern as the Marine Corps liaison

man on Capitol Hill is the Corps itself and how well it comes out in the annual wrangle on the Hill over various military money bills.

The Corps comes out well.

Bonner denies he is a lobbyist, although when pressed he was unable to spell out specifically how his work with the Congress was different from that of other lobbyists. He likes to think of himself as an expeditor of matters concerning the Corps and is especially proud of the work he did on the promotion for the Assistant Commandant, who, at the time, was General Lewis Walt.

The Marine Corps drafted a bill and sent it along to the House Armed Services Committee for action, finding there, as always, a warm welcome from the chairman and his chief counsel. As presented, the bill (H.R. 3832, Ninety-First Congress, First Session) stated: "Be it enacted by the Senate and House of Representatives in Congress assembled, That the grade of the Assistant Commandant of the Marine Corps is that of general so long as such office is held by the present incumbent."

On February 3, 1969, the committee met in Room 2118 of the Rayburn Building, with Chairman Rivers presiding, to take up the matter of the upgrading of the Assistant Commandant. The bill to effect the change was introduced for the Marines by Chairman Rivers, who agreed with them that the "Assistant Commandant should enjoy a status equal to his counterparts." But Chairman Rivers didn't like one aspect of the bill as proposed by the Marines. As worded, it would apply only to the present occupant, General Walt. "Why should it be confined to the present occupant?" Rivers asked. "This to me is ridiculous, and I hope the committee amends it."

The committee amended it.

Whereas Chairman Rivers is always ready to come to the defense of the Defense Department, he is also ready to remind the Department of Defense who its friends are. On March 27, 1969, at the start of hearings on a military appropriations measure, Rivers reminded the newly appointed Secretary of Defense, Melvin Laird, that "this committee is the only official spokesman for the Department of Defense on the floor." He also made it plain that the Department of Defense would not have as many friends in the Senate Armed Services Committee as it had in the House.

"I can tell you this," Rivers said, "we can do a much better job than they can do in the other body. You have too much opposition there."

Rivers is deeply concerned about opposition to the military establishment, as the following exchange among Rivers, Laird, and General Blandford indicates, from the same March 27 hearings:

> THE CHAIRMAN: We are quite disturbed—I am, at least—over what was mentioned: the growing menace of the military-industrial complex. They have taken General Eisenhower's words and twisted them all over the place. All these newspapers are editorializing it. We hear it on the radio. We see it on the TV screen, of these unknowledgeable people.
>
> It is a conspiracy, in my opinion, going on today against our military. If you don't know that, I would advise you to look into it, because there is a conspiracy to downgrade and make our military absolutely powerless to meet our commitments as well as the security of this country.
>
> Do you make that same observation from what you picked up?
>
> SECRETARY LAIRD: Mr. Chairman, I think the remarks of former President Eisenhower have been—

THE CHAIRMAN: Distorted, I think.

SECRETARY LAIRD: [continuing] Distorted.

THE CHAIRMAN: I think they have been distorted. I don't think he meant it in the context these people are using it.

SECRETARY LAIRD: I had the opportunity of meeting with General Eisenhower quite recently and of briefing him almost on a weekly basis. There was no person to my knowledge who had a greater interest in protecting the national security of this country and who realized the necessity for giving the highest priority to our defense and national security needs if we did want to maintain peace in the world. He felt this was most important, and he became a peace President because he believed in building enough strength in the United States to deter war.

At this point, General Earl Wheeler, Chairman of the Joint Chiefs of Staff, also appearing before the committee, joined the discussion:

GENERAL WHEELER: May I make a comment, Mr. Chairman?

THE CHAIRMAN: Yes, certainly.

GENERAL WHEELER: If you really read the farewell radio and television address to the American people by President Eisenhower, delivered from his office, on January 17, 1961, you will find the following words. This is on page 1037 of Public Papers of the Presidents:

A vital element in keeping the peace is our Military Establishment. Our arms must be mighty, ready for instant action, so no potential aggressor may be tempted to risk his own destruction.

This is all a very interesting dissertation from my viewpoint. Then comes a short paragraph that has always been quoted:

In the councils of our Government we must guard against the acquisition of unwarranted influence whether sought or unsought, by the military-industrial complex. The potential for the disastrous rise of misplaced power exists and will persist.

However, if you go over to the next page, page 1039—and in between, I might add, there are several interesting paragraphs—you will find this:

The prospect of domination of the Nation's scholars by Federal employment, project allocations, and the power of money is ever present—and is gravely to be regarded. Yet, in holding scientific research and discovery in respect, as we should, we must also be alert to the equal and opposite danger that public policy could itself become the captive of a scientific-technological elite.

It is the task of statesmanship to mold, to balance, and to integrate these and other forces, new and old, within the principles of our democratic system—ever aiming toward the supreme goals of our free society.

In other words, what I am pointing out, Mr. Chairman, is that President Eisenhower's statement was taken completely out of context and has been used, I think, in a most dangerous and inappropriate way.

MR. BLANDFORD: In other words, he warned about another takeover too.

GENERAL WHEELER: He did.

THE CHAIRMAN: He surely did.

MR. BLANDFORD: Nobody bothered to mention it —the new left wing.

Exchanges such as this one leave no doubt in the Pentagon about the friendliness of the House Armed Services Committee under Chairman Rivers, and the officials of the Defense Department can only be cheered by Rivers' words to Secretary Laird in his first appearance before the committee when Rivers expressed the hope that "this is going to be the beginning of a long, happy and cooperative effort between the two of us."

The Armed Services Committee has too long been concerned solely with the problems of the Defense Department and not enough with the problems and welfare of the enlisted men and women in the services. For too long the main concern of the House Armed Services Committee has been to protect and play along with the Pentagon, at the expense of the ordinary serviceman. Individual appeals by men in the service find little sympathy from the committee and, as often as not, are simply referred to the proper office in the Pentagon for disposition. Investigations are not investigations at all, but junkets. Hard questions are not asked. Sugar coating is amply applied. The committee functions as a guardian of the military when it should be its chief antagonist. Instead of barging in and asking questions at the Pentagon, the House Armed Services Committee has posted "off limits" signs.

This too-cozy relationship between the Armed Services Committee and the Pentagon would be regrettable in and of itself were it not for the fact that the committee's enormous power over other members of Congress were not so unbridled. A Congressman who is deeply affected and concerned about a letter he receives from a young man in the service alleging brutality or other maltreatment finds that if he speaks out against such conditions, he will be subjected to reprisal or threat of reprisal from the very committee that should be championing the cause of the ordinary GI.

Quite clearly, there is merit in a proposal to establish a separate body to hear and investigate grievances voiced by servicemen. Whether that body should be another committee of the Congress or whether it should be outside of Congress is quite another matter. Representative Biaggi proposed legislation that would put military justice into civilian hands by establishing a commission on military justice. This would consist of five civilians and five representatives of each branch of the armed forces. All would be appointed by the President. The commission would have investigative and punitive powers.

This proposal, although admirable and although providing a basis for a discussion about this vital matter, had little chance of passage even on the day it was introduced because of the power of the House Committee on Armed Services, which claims jurisdiction over all legislation affecting the military.

Biaggi stated that "the military machinery governing the process of complaints from enlisted men is inadequate, obsolete, and in many respects, grossly unfair."

There are inadequacies in our system of military justice and they should be corrected, but first we must deal with what has become, unfortunately, a major stumbling block on the road to improving these inadequacies in our armed forces—the present House Armed Services Committee. How to accomplish this is a question that the Congress must decide, but it is clear that nothing will be done until the Congress initiates reforms so that no one man, no single committee, can have and use the awesome power that now resides in the Armed Services Committee.

Biaggi's attempts to modify injustices are laudable and should be pursued with vigor by those who agree, as we do, that it is immaterial whether there be one case of injustice or a thousand, as Biaggi stated. "There is not room for even one," Biaggi said in a House speech. "If we have sadism, it should be eliminated. We are dealing with the military and with hundreds of thousands of people. No one would dare stand here and defend all of them or the conduct of all. For those who would whitewash the military problems at the expense of our enlisted men, I serve notice here and now that I will continue to do all in my power to give human dignity and pride to the enlisted men."

CHAPTER NINE

THE BRIG RATS

Our primary mission here is rehabilitative in nature.
Commanding Officer, the Parris Island brig

In the heart of the Parris Island Recruit Training Depot stands a building dating back to the last decade of the last century, a sturdy but worn old building used as a brig, or, as the Marines prefer to call it, a correction center. On the average, seventy Marines are housed in the brig at any one time. For them and the Corps, this is the last resort in the long and rugged ritual by which the Marines try to turn a young man into a Marine. Here are the ones who didn't make it and probably never will. These are the guys who went over the hill, or tried to; the ones who wouldn't submit to the harassment and the "thumping"; the eight balls, malcontents, and losers. They have committed crimes of various kinds and are either on their way out of the Corps with bad conduct discharges or simply passing time in a way station before serving longer sentences in a federal prison. The brig separates its inmates according to their status. Recruits who have erred but who may still be fashioned into Marines are kept away from the ones on whom the Marines have given up.

Few people get a look at the inside of a Marine brig, and until this book, no one was ever permitted to take a tape recorder inside, to sit down with inmates, and to interview them. If by our insistence on being allowed this privilege the Marines will, in the future, permit regular examination of its brigs, we are pleased. Because we believe that no aspect of life in the armed services should be beyond the view of the American people, we pressed for the opportunity to interview prisoners in the Parris Island brig. The material obtained was necessarily limited because those prisoners we hoped to interview remained suspicious. A few, however, seized the opportunity.

Naturally reluctant to open its brig to reporters, the Marines at Parris Island insisted on rigorous guidelines for the tour of the facility and the interviews, but reporters look with disdain on guidelines arbitrarily set down by governmental authorities, and so the guidelines were ignored, stretched, or "negotiated." The fact that they were negotiated with several different officers led to a happy confusion among them, so that these officers were never really very clear on what the guidelines were.

Men in the brig are not allowed to smoke, so as each man to be interviewed came into the room, we offered him a cigarette. Base and brig officers who were present bridled at this gesture, although Public Information Officer Arnold good-naturedly saw the gesture for what it was, a ploy, a technique to get the inmate's confidence. Each man was also seated so that he did not face any of the officers in the room, one of which was the man's legal defense counsel. All the defense counsels were consulted prior to the interviews, and each of them met privately with his client to discuss the man's rights.

We picked four men at random. Of these four, three agreed to be interviewed. The first was a twenty-year-old recruit from Macon, Georgia, who had gone on an unauthorized absence. He was obviously nervous and reluctant to talk:

> AUTHORS: How is it in the brig? You can say whatever you want.
> PRISONER: Not that bad really, sir.
> AUTHORS: How are you treated?
> PRISONER: Could be better. It's no picnic here, sir. I'm doing my best to get out.
> AUTHORS: When you say it's not a picnic, are you talking about the rules, or do the people go beyond the rules?
> PRISONER: I'm just doing what I can do to stay out of trouble so I can get out of the Marine Corps.
> AUTHORS: Are you saying that sometimes somebody says you're not going by the rules? And that you get punished for it?
> PRISONER: Yes, sir. Get punished for nothin' sometimes.
> AUTHORS: Can you give an example?
> PRISONER: This is a recruit brig and they try to get you to go back to duty. They bend the rules once in a while.

The recruit would not be drawn out further. He plainly was acutely aware of the officers standing behind him.

The second man interviewed was also reluctant to go into any details of his life in the brig except to say, significantly, "You'll be leaving here, sir. I have to stay."

Private Charles Teady, Jr., the third inmate interviewed, talked readily:

TEADY: My lawyer has advised me what to say. Down here they got some smart lawyers on this island. They know their business. I feel I got a pretty good lawyer. He told me if I want to say something, say it. If I want to mention my name, mention it. You got my permission. You can mention my name if you want to. You can tell it for publication.

AUTHORS: [To an officer] Colonel, if this man is willing to talk about his particular case, can we do that?

COLONEL: That's up to him and his counsel.

AUTHORS: I'd like to talk to you about the specific violation that you're charged with. Would you talk about that?

TEADY: Yes, sir, I don't have any secrets.

LEGAL COUNSEL: For the record, while the machine is running I will make a statement. Private Teady, we have discussed this this afternoon. This is your decision. You have had my advice. Your case is not completed, and I tell you again, you have the right not to speak. At this point you may exercise your own judgment.

TEADY: Yes, sir.

LEGAL COUNSEL: Is there any question you have before the interview continues? Or do you want to talk to me about it before we go on?

TEADY: No, sir.

AUTHORS: I assume we can go on with it?

TEADY: Yes, sir.

AUTHORS: How long were you UA [unauthorized absence]?

TEADY: I was UA May fourth to September twenty-fourth, sir.

AUTHORS: Why did you go UA?

TEADY: I got tired of the Marine Corps, sir.

AUTHORS: How long had you been in at that time?

TEADY: April eighth to May fourth.

AUTHORS: What did you get tired of?

TEADY: I got tired of the way people were treatin' me. I just got tired.

AUTHORS: How were they treating you?

TEADY: They stress that discipline a little too much at times. I was put in Motivation. I don't know what I was put in there for. So I just left. UA.

AUTHORS: What did they tell you you were put in Motivation for?

TEADY: They told me for my own benefit.

AUTHORS: How long were you in Motivation?

TEADY: Three days, sir.

AUTHORS: How did you get out? How did you go?

TEADY: UA, sir. I'm not saying how I got out, but I left.

AUTHORS: You didn't go in the water?

TEADY: I just went UA, left the island.

AUTHORS: Because it's pretty rough getting off this place.

TEADY: Yes, sir, it is.

AUTHORS: Was it rough for you getting off?

TEADY: No, sir. I got off.

AUTHORS: Where did you go?

TEADY: Home. Went home and got married.

AUTHOR: Were you apprehended, or did you give yourself up?

TEADY: Apprehended, sir. The FBI, sir.

AUTHORS: Did you know they were going to get you?

TEADY: They get you sooner or later.

AUTHORS: How was the court-martial you had? Fair?

TEADY: Yes, sir.

AUTHORS: And the sentence?

TEADY: Five months, sir. BCD.

AUTHORS: When you get through here, you will get a bad-conduct discharge?

TEADY: Yes, sir.

AUTHORS: How do you feel about that?

TEADY: Well, it's all what you make out of a BCD. You can make it hard on yourself, you can make it light on yourself. You can let that BCD get you down, or you can make something out of yourself. You don't have to be a man to go in the Marine Corps and let them make a man out of you. You can do it yourself. I'm a man already.

AUTHORS: Were you a man when you came in the Marines?

TEADY: Yes, sir.

AUTHORS: Did you know it then?

TEADY: Yes, sir.

AUTHORS: Why did you join?

TEADY: I didn't join, I was drafted.

AUTHORS: Were you pretty bitter about that?

TEADY: I wasn't too happy about it.

AUTHORS: If you had a chance to do it all over again, what would happen?

TEADY: I would have gone UA sooner or later. Would have got a discharge. It would have been the same. Nothing is goin' to change a man inside. A man's already made up.

There is no question that the Marine Corps experience had left this young man deeply embittered. Each attempt by the Corps to "motivate" him had succeeded only in further alienating him. As he left the interview, there was little doubt that he would have a rough time of it until he got his BCD. Obviously, he was prepared for it.

At the time of this visit, the brig housed eighty-eight prisoners, somewhat higher than the average figure. Most of these men are confined to one huge, barnlike room in which are all their facilities—showers, toilets, bunks, and mess area. But when the weather is good, the inmates spend most of their time outside in a large, fenced recreation yard. There are no guard towers looking down, and the guards do not carry weapons. A good deal of the time spent outdoors is also devoted to working on the island, street cleaning, and maintenance work.

The brig does have cells. One type is used for maximum-security prisoners and houses only one inmate at a time. A second type is somewhat larger and is equipped to house four men at a time.

For recruits sent to the brig, regular training exercises are maintained so that they will be up to date with their training schedules when their term in the brig has ended. For these men, the rigors of recruit training are compounded by the loss of even limited freedom. In at least one instance they are deprived of something other recruits are permitted. A part of every recruit's day is set aside for him to use his own way, and in this period he is allowed to read. For the recruit in the brig, the only reading permitted is the reading of Marine Corps manuals. It may seem a small deprivation, but for an imprisoned man whose last freedom has been taken away in the midst of the hardships of recruit training, it seems an unnecessary and even cruel regulation.

Recruits in the brig eat the same food as other recruits, and it is good food. As a disciplinary measure some recruits may be put on a restricted diet. According to Navy regulations, the restricted diet consists of 2,100 calories a day served in three meals. These may *not* include meat, eggs, butter, sweets, desserts, and seasonings. Water is the only drink allowed. This extremely harsh diet will consist mainly of cereals, potatoes, and bread. There is no limitation under the Navy regulation on the number of days a man may be required to live on this diet.

In addition to the disciplinary diet, a prisoner may be subjected to disciplinary segregation. The regulations state that this measure "shall be imposed only on extremely recalcitrant offenders." Again, the period of time is variable. "Individual prisoners differ greatly in the time required to gain their cooperation. Therefore disciplinary segregation should not be ordered for a fixed period of time but may be terminated as soon as the prisoner demonstrates that segregation has served its purpose," a Parris Island brig officer explained.

The length of time is supposed to be set by the commanding officer, and only he is allowed to order it. In practice, in many Marine brigs the determination is made by individual guards on their own, without consulting officers.

If brutality and maltreatment of recruits is difficult to uncover under normal circumstances, it is virtually impossible to discover it when a man is confined to the brig. A Marine who feels he has been maltreated may, as many of the cases in this book demonstrate, tell about those instances in letters home. Mail into and out of the brig is censored. Brutality and inmate maltreatment exists, however, and some Marine brigs are notorious for it.

An FBI agent recounted an instance in which a Marine whom he arrested for being UA wept openly, begging the agent not to send him to the Great Lakes Naval Station because he knew that he would be savagely beaten by guards in the brig when he returned. A young Canadian who had joined the U.S. Marines, only to go UA, described the treatment that he could expect if he returned to his duty as an MP at the Philadelphia Navy Base. "First thing the MP's will do is make me take off my clothes. Then they'll make me lean on my hands against the wall while they beat me with a belt. I'll get kicked and punched. All of that before I'm even turned over to an officer for official punishment," he explained. He returned to Canada, abandoning his Marine career forever.

Perhaps the most notorious Marine brig is the one at Camp Pendleton, California. This prison was subjected to very intensive public scrutiny as the result of disclosures in newspapers and magazines of rampant brutality, racism, and sexual abuses. The *Nation* charged that the Pendleton brig was a modern Devil's Island where men were brutalized and forced to live in "primitive conditions." But the most damaging reports of all were published in *Life* magazine in an article by Jack Fincher. He alleged that prisoners were sometimes isolated in private rooms at the whim of guards and exercised to the limit of their endurance and then were beaten; that guards bound prisoners' heads like mummies to keep them quiet; that prisoners were handcuffed to a chain-link ceiling and left hanging for hours; and that prisoners were confined to the "ice box," a cagelike building that could be closed up to become unbearably hot during the day and opened to the ocean-wet cold at night.

Camp Pendleton is a huge complex on the Pacific, halfway between San Diego and Los Angeles, and borders on President Nixon's West Coast White House at San Clemente. Within the confines of Pendleton stands the brig, a collection of tin-roofed buildings that at times have handled fourteen thousand prisoners in less than two years. Many of those prisoners were Marines who had gone UA to avoid being shipped to Vietnam.

Its proximity to Vietnam gives Pendleton a total load of court-martial cases far beyond those of other Marine bases. The West Coast, namely Pendleton, is the mouth of the funnel through which all Marines being transferred to the West Pacific flow. In calendar year 1968, Pendleton had 2,997 courts-martial.

The brig facilities at Pendleton are in terrible condition, far worse than the brig at Parris Island, which is housed in a building nearly eighty years old. The Pendleton brig is a combination of converted World War II barracks, Quonset huts, and temporary metal buildings, the piecemeal construction of which has resulted in an unwieldy complex covering more than twenty acres. According to the Marine Corps, "The brig has a capacity of 392 men on a normal basis of 72 square feet per man. It receives large numbers of stragglers and UA personnel from all over the West Coast, as well as supporting the units located at the base. In 1969 the brig population continued to rise despite efforts to alleviate the situation."

The Marines went before the House Armed Services Committee in July, 1969, to appeal for funds for the building of new brig facilities at Pendleton.

"This is the largest brig in the Marine Corps," testified Brigadier General William C. Chip, Assistant Quarter Master General, "and, as I understand, the largest brig in the Navy as well."

"Are you bragging or apologizing?" asked Chairman L. Mendel Rivers.

"We are not bragging about it, sir. It is the situation we are in on the West Coast at the present time. Camp Pendleton brig has to take stragglers and unauthorized personnel from all over the West Coast."

Committee Member Durward G. Hall asked, "General, do you need this entire amount for this fancy brig? Admitted that what you are living in is impossible, and what you are working with defies security and proper custody and everything else, do you need over two and a half million dollars for an eight-story brig?"

Representative Hall then went on to state it was his

belief that it's a bad thing to take "all the austerity out of
the Marine Corps." He added, "We have got to continue
to build men. I am not sure that you would build one after
you've got him in the brig. But be that as it may, this is an
awful price to pay for a jail, or even a modern brig, with
all-security conditions."

General Chip told the committee, almost pleadingly,
"this does include mess facilities, administrative spaces,
and also makes provision for the required guard facilities."

Nodding his head patiently, Hall stated, "I want to be
sure, and I wish you could reassure me, the standards you
are trying to come up to aren't standards set by some
dreamer with long hair down in the Health, Education
and Welfare Department building."

The words from Representative Hall would have been
small comfort to a man enmeshed in the horrors of the
Pendleton brig, especially if the man thought that if he
could just get a letter about his troubles off to a Congressman, his plight would be bettered. The kind of thinking that
worried about the Marine Corps losing its austerity because
it wanted to replace buildings three decades old at the Pendleton brig with a modest, modern two-story brig is, however, typical of the mentality that has sat in seats of
influence of the House Committee on Armed Services, a
committee which shows a shocking lack of interest in the
plight of enlisted personnel.

Publication of stories alleging brutality at Pendleton
in *Nation* and *Life* and resulting public indignation forced
the House Armed Services Committee to look into the brig
at Pendleton.

The commandant of the Camp Pendleton Marine base
admitted that there had been cases of brutality by guards
against inmates. Major General Donn J. Robertson called
a news conference in September, 1969, in the wake of an
announcement by House Armed Services Committee Chair-

man Rivers that the situation would be probed. Taking newsmen on a tour of the brig, which at this time housed 796 prisoners in space designed for a maximum of 300, General Robertson confirmed cases of brutality alleged in the magazines and also admitted that there had been prisoner disturbances at the brig in January and June in which forty-six men were injured.

True to his word, Chairman Rivers sent a small group of investigators to Pendleton to make an initial probe of the brig. They visited the brig and dutifully turned in their report to the committee chairman.

In December, 1969, nearly three months after the committee investigators visited Pendleton, a South Carolina newspaper reported that the staff had found that black prisoners had made "slaves" of white prisoners through a "kangaroo court." This court allegedly ordered beatings for whites who resisted the "black supremacy" organization established at the brig along the lines of the Black Panthers. "Under threat of beatings, the white 'slaves' are required to perform menial tasks and in some cases submit to homosexual attack," the newspaper said.

Rushing into the headlines, Rivers stated that the matter would be investigated by the same subcommittee he had established to investigate racial brawls at Camp Lejeune. In its report (discussed in detail in a previous chapter) on that situation, the subcommittee headed by Representative William J. Randall recommended that the racial problem facing the Corps be left with the Corps to correct. But significantly, on the charge that blacks had enslaved whites at Pendleton, Chairman Rivers decided that the Marines were not able to straighten out the matter themselves and that his committee was going "to assist the Marines."

In fact, the situation had been largely corrected long before Rivers made his headline-grabbing announcement of another investigation. One of his own staff told United Press International that "corrective action was taken almost immediately. Inexperienced guards were replaced with experienced men. More guards were brought in. Guards were given more training."

It was not until February 26, 1970—five months after public disclosure of the scandalous conditions at the Pendleton brig forced the Armed Services Committee to send investigators—that the Randall subcommittee made its report on its findings. The report warned that violent racial clashes would continue in all military installations unless the armed forces significantly upgraded the quality of both their facilities and their correctional staffs. "The classic formula for turbulence is to overpopulate an ill-suited confinement facility and then assign a staff that is undermanned, unmotivated, and low in morale"—cheeringly hopeful words that make one wonder if there has been some sudden change of attitude by a committee that less than two years earlier seriously questioned the need to spend $2.5 million for a new brig at Pendleton and then almost grudgingly appropriated the money. The Randall subcommittee's eleven-page report on Pendleton's brig said the situation was "much improved," with a reduction in the prisoner population from 806 at the end of 1968 to 363 as of mid-January, 1970. The report also listed an increase in the number of guards and administrators and an improvement in facilities until work can begin on the new brig facility. "There was sufficient evidence to indicate that there did exist at certain times domination by blacks in controlling certain huts and some segments of prison life through kangaroo courts and threats of bodily harm," the report stated. "There were incidents of servitude involving Caucasian prisoners. The subcommittee heard no direct evidence of forced homosexual conduct; however, there were indications that such activities took place in isolated instances."

The Randall subcommittee also said it learned of two occasions in which a prisoner was spread-eagled on a chain fence. Another prisoner had his mouth taped shut in a way that made it difficult to breathe. The famous "icebox" had, indeed, existed. Guards, had, indeed, beaten prisoners.

These conditions, the report stated, had been corrected, and it confidently reported that when guard mistreatment was again uncovered, it was promptly ended and the offenders disciplined.

Comforting words. But their utterance was made possible not because the House Armed Services Committee pursued with doggedness its mandate to oversee the armed forces in all aspects of their activities, but because public disclosures in two magazines had put a spotlight on those horrible conditions, and then, apparently, only because there was evidence that blacks were oppressing whites.

One wonders if the committee's chairman would have been as eager to unearth the deplorable affairs at Pendleton if their racial aspect had been reversed. And one wonders too whether the committee will exercise the same diligence in probing the conditions that exist in virtually every other military prison operated by the armed forces in this country and around the world.

A further reminder of the problems in the Pendleton brig came on August 26, 1970, when a four-hour melee described by a Pendleton spokesman as "a race riot" broke out. When the riot was over, fifteen blacks were under arrest. Two whites and six blacks were treated for injuries. At the time the number of men in the brig was about four hundred.

Prisons, even in civilian life, are the stepchildren of society. Their inmates are behind walls, shut off from the rest of us, and their needs are not readily seen.

One does not expect to find the nation's ideal citizens in its jails and prisons, and the Marine Corps does not find its best men in its brigs. A certain number of the men in a brig are men who would probably be in civilian jails if they were civilians, but by and large most of the men in brigs at any given time are those charged with unauthorized absences. At Pendleton most of the UA cases were men who decided they did not want to go to Vietnam. Many of them went UA repeatedly. The purpose of putting these men into the brig was not to correct or rehabilitate them, but to coerce them. They were expected to come to the conclusion that it would be better for them to be in Vietnam than in the Pendleton brig. This atmosphere naturally breeds brutalities.

Brutality in a brig is as illegal officially as it is in boot camp, and it is just as hard, if not harder, to prove. It is always a case of a prisoner's word against a guard's. When this situation involves a guard who has been to Vietnam and a prisoner who is trying to avoid going, the potential for brutality undiscovered and brutality unpunished is that much greater.

Many brig guards are ordinary Marines, not men especially trained for corrective work. These men bring to the brigs an attitude that those in their care are there because they are a discredit to the Corps, cowards, or worse and that slugging them once in a while can't do any harm. There are many who may agree with a Marine officer quoted by Jack Fincher in *Life* who reportedly said that the way to clear up the problem of Marine brigs was to choose a Marine of the month who would be taken out and shot until there weren't any more men left in the brig.

An atmosphere of oppression is created in which it is hoped the prisoner will rebel by striking out at a guard. "They want you to hit them," a prisoner at the Brooklyn brig stated, " 'cause if you hit 'em you're in hot water."

There is a system by which inmates can complain about

their treatment. They can fill out a charge sheet, and on this may allege maltreatment on the part of guards. A prisoner at the Brooklyn brig laughed at the idea of the charge sheet. He said, "When we write up a charge sheet on them for profane language in front of a prisoner, the charge does not go through. But the minute they write up a charge on us, on anything [snapping his fingers], right on through and we get sent down to segregation."

Segregation is much like solitary confinement in a civilian prison. It is used in Marine brigs for two reasons: to maintain a man's security or safety, and for discipline. Security segregation is given to those men who are risks, either of suicide, escape, drugs, or homosexuality. Disciplinary segregation is for troublemakers.

"A man can only be given disciplinary segregation by the colonel," said a Marine officer at the Brooklyn brig, an assertion that turned out to be more propaganda than fact inasmuch as at least one prisoner was taken into disciplinary segregation while the authors were touring the brig at a time when the colonel, supposedly to be the only one able to authorize that punishment, was not on the premises.

In brigs, as at training depots, what the Marines tell you and what is actually the case are sometimes quite different.

Similarly, what a prisoner will tell you and what is the truth are sometimes different.

Seeing one of the authors touring the Brooklyn brig with a tape recorder running, a prisoner in segregation shouted at the accompanying Marine officer, "How come all this immediate concern for a prisoner just because this man is here? All of a sudden everything is jumping. Never seen this before, people coming in here and asking you your problems. What's going on?"

"Have you seen me here every day?" asked the officer.

"Not every day, but you try to be here," the prisoner replied.

"How many times this week have you been taken out of that cell to go to dental or sick bay or gone someplace?" the officer asked.

"Not once," snapped the prisoner from inside his cell.

"I don't believe you," replied the officer.

"I put in a request sheet for dental last Friday, first day I was here, and—"

"Let's get this straight," said the officer firmly. "Just because this gentleman is here with his microphone, we're not going to lie to you and we aren't going to lie to him. You're not the only people in this facility nor in the Naval station, and when the dental people can take you, they will. But they are not going to drop everything because a prisoner says so."

The problem with the man and his demand to go to the dentist was not so much that his teeth needed attention as it was that he wanted to get out of his segregation cell, even if it meant a trip to the dentist's chair.

A man's length of time in segregation, either protective or disciplinary, depends on his particular case. "On disciplinary segregation," it was explained, "the man's conduct tells us when he comes out of there. If he wants to be in there, just be a bad ass, he can stay there for quite a while. If he doesn't, if he behaves himself and says yes, sir, I've learned my lesson, he can get out in a few days. He judges himself."

In the special jargon of the Marine brig system, prisoners are called confinees. It is a relatively new term. Repeatedly, the men in charge of brigs had to catch themselves as they started to say prisoners, changing to the newer, nicer word.

There is nothing nice about a prison of any kind. Military prisons, because of their austerity and because of a tendency to avoid spending time and money on their improvement, are often among the worst prisons in this country. The Pendleton brig was referred to in one account of its horrors as being worse than the infamous Andersonville prison of the Civil War. Brigs in the Marine Corps vary in quality. Pendleton was listed among the worst because it had more prisoners, more problems. The problems of the brig at Parris Island, which handles mostly recruits, are far different from the Pendleton problems. The location of a brig will have a considerable effect on its nature. Parris Island's correction center, isolated from the rest of the world because it is surrounded by the sprawling Marine training base, need not worry about having to cope with the problems Pendleton faced because it was the mouth of the Vietnam funnel. Nor do the officers and guards at Parris Island face the problem that daily confronts the officers and guards at the Marine brig located in the heart of New York's Bedford-Stuyvesant ghetto— drugs, a contamination that has spilled over into the U.S. Naval hospital and the Marine brig.

"Who do we have to know to get drugs?" a prisoner was asked.

"Just be a Marine, I guess, and eventually you'll find out," he replied.

CHAPTER TEN

THE TURNED-ON BRIG

*But now, Jesus, here we are, right in the
middle of Bedford-Stuyvesant.*
An officer of the Brooklyn brig

If ever a military prison were located in the wrong place,
it is the Naval brig containing Marine and Navy prisoners
on the fifth floor of the Naval Command Headquarters on
Flushing Avenue in the heart of Brooklyn's Bedford-
Stuyvesant ghetto. Directly opposite the almost-abandoned
Brooklyn Navy Yard, the facility was scheduled for closing until the Vietnam war required its continued operation.

The Brooklyn brig is contaminated by narcotics to such
an extent that the commander of the Marine barracks,
Lieutenant Colonel Francis W. Tief, would not even guess
about the scope of the problem. At one time, of twenty-
seven Marines awaiting courts-martial in his brig, seventeen of them were charged with narcotics violations.

There is no kind of narcotic not available to men in
the Brooklyn brig and the adjoining St. Alban's U.S.
Naval Hospital.

In an interview with Representative Biaggi a twenty-

year-old Marine from Syracuse, New York, who was confined to the Brooklyn brig on a narcotics charge stated that
he first began using drugs when he was a patient at St.
Alban's:

BIAGGI: You became a drug addict when you were
at St. Alban's Hospital?
MARINE: Not really a drug addict, but I started
on drugs. I had problems when I was there. It's
easy to get drugs in the hospital.
BIAGGI: Where did you get them from? Civilian
personnel?
MARINE: I believe some was from civilian per-
sonnel.
BIAGGI: Military personnel?
MARINE: Yes.
BIAGGI: Did you pay for them?
MARINE: Yes.
BIAGGI: What did you pay?
MARINE: Three, four dollars. As high as six dol-
lars.
BIAGGI: Where did you get the money?
MARINE: From my military pay. I had nothin' else
to spend it on.
BIAGGI: What were you in the hospital for?
MARINE: I hurt my knee in Vietnam.
BIAGGI: What is wrong with your knee?
MARINE: I had one kneecap removed. After it
was removed they kept sending me back to duty.
BIAGGI: Are they selling drugs here in the brig?
MARINE: Yes, this place is.
BIAGGI: Where?
MARINE: Downstairs. On the fourth deck.
BIAGGI: How do you know?
MARINE: How do I know? I bought drugs here.

From many people.
BIAGGI: How much do you pay here?
MARINE: Five dollars.
BIAGGI: For what?
MARINE: Heroin.
BIAGGI: Who was selling the drugs?
MARINE: Marine personnel here.
BIAGGI: Is this done openly, or what?
MARINE: Yes, a lot of people do it, it seems to me, openly.
BIAGGI: How are the narcotics coming into the Naval base here? Do you know?
MARINE: I don't know. People just go out.
BIAGGI: If I went down to the fourth deck now, could I buy narcotics?
MARINE: If you knew certain people.
BIAGGI: Who do I have to know?
MARINE: Just be a Marine, I guess, and eventually you'll find out.
BIAGGI: There must be some seller there. You can tell us.
MARINE: Everybody's got the drugs. It seems like everybody I know uses drugs.
BIAGGI: In this place?
MARINE: Yes. Ever since I came to St. Alban's. It seems that every ward I've been in, somebody, a lot of people were using drugs. *I'm telling you, everybody is using drugs around here.*

The story was the same with other prisoners in the Brooklyn brig. A nineteen-year-old sailor from Brooklyn, serving time for being UA for sixty days:

BIAGGI: Do you use narcotics?
SAILOR: Not here. While I was outside, yes.

BIAGGI: Can you get narcotics here at the Navy base in Brooklyn?

SAILOR: It can be done. They have it downstairs on the fourth deck.

BIAGGI: Who is selling narcotics there?

SAILOR: I don't know. I just saw it being passed on.

BIAGGI: What kind of narcotics?

SAILOR: Heroin.

The drugs openly available at the Brooklyn Naval facility come from the neighborhood, a sprawling, decaying ghetto in the heart of Brooklyn, bounded by Bedford and Stuyvesant Streets, the scene of racial unrest and one of the high crime areas of New York City. An officer of the brig told Biaggi, "It's the neighborhood more than anything else. Pretty easy to get around this area, as I'm sure you are aware if you took a look around. It's quite easy for these boys to make buys in any number of places. A lot of the men started using drugs elsewhere, Vietnam primarily."

How can a man in the brig get drugs from the streets? A piece of string and a bedspring provide a ready tool, as this interview with a young prisoner suggests:

MARINE: They said I was trying to bring drugs into the brig. I wasn't tryin' to bring no drugs into the brig. I had a piece of string, you know what I mean? And I had a spring attached to it, but I didn't have it outta the window, you know? I was just foolin' around with it. They say I was puttin' it outta the window, the time they seen me, but I was just standin' there talkin' to my friend....

When cash is not available to buy drugs, they can be obtained by barter:

BIAGGI: Do you take drugs?

MARINE: No.

BIAGGI: Can you buy drugs in this place?

MARINE: They say it's brought into here by sentries for prisoners.

BIAGGI: Brought in by sentries and sold to prisoners?

MARINE: If you have a certain amount of cigarettes in your possession you can get—

BIAGGI: I don't understand the relationship.

MARINE: If you don't have the money, cigarettes act like money.

Another young Marine interviewed by the authors was awaiting a court-martial for possession of 1,400 sticks of marijuana, which he was alleged to be selling at St. Alban's Hospital, where he was a patient for a knee injury. This was not the same man interviewed by Biaggi.

A man awaiting disposition of his case at the Brooklyn brig is first interviewed by the brig commander, Lieutenant Colonel Tief, during his "office hours." Admitting that his greatest problem with prisoners in his brig is narcotics, Tief first of all blames the location of the brig for much of the problem. When the brig was previously located inside the now closed Brooklyn Navy Yard, he was able to maintain considerable control over it through stringent screening processes. "Honestly, I don't know of another prison that has the same physical setup that we do," he stated. "Let's face it, we're one block in the middle of a city neighborhood. If they could find another place for this setup, we'd be a thousand times better off. In fact, I look at the Coast Guard over at Governor's Island, and it's really as though the grass were greener. It's a military operation. There's space, there's no involvement with civilians the way we are here, right on top of each other. Before, when we were inside the Yard, it was a different proposition. We had a military atmosphere. But now, Jesus, here we are, right in the middle of Bedford-Stuyvesant."

At his "office hours," Tief deals sternly with the narcotics problem. He "goes the limit" on pushers, recommending a general court-martial as well as a prison sentence. Heavy users he recommends to special courts-martial. For other users, not on hard narcotics, he suggests administrative action, either an undesirable or a general discharge. In the latter case, he talks to the parents of the young Marines. If they guarantee that their sons will undergo a civilian rehabilitation program, he will recommend general discharge by reason of unsuitability.

Coming into his command in an average month are 182 men, most of them charged with unauthorized absence. Aiding Tief is Chief Warrant Officer Leason McCoy, an old-timer. He came to the Brooklyn brig about the same time as Tief, three years ago. At the time of the writing of this book both men were awaiting transfers.

McCoy says the job of a corrections officer in the Marines has three equally important aspects: (1) the security of the prisoners, (2) solving the problems of prisoners, and (3) acculturation back into Marine life.

Both Tief and McCoy confessed to some dismay over the Marine Corps's insistence on the use of a new vocabulary, referring to brigs as correctional centers and prisoners as confinees.

The Marine command in Brooklyn has two highly trained counselors, both chiefs in the Navy at the time of the writing of this book. These men assist in solving the problems that may have led Marines to go UA. "If we can't solve a confinee's problems, it's our failure," says McCoy. "These problems might be a girl friend pregnant, or no money at home, or other family problems."

At "office hours," Tief, McCoy, and another officer or Marine NCO interview the men who have been brought into the brig and make determinations on the disposition of their cases. These interviews are not unlike arraignments or preliminary hearings in civilian magistrates' courts. The chief difference is that a Marine never goes free on bail. He is detained until his case comes to trial.

The authors sat in on a typical session of "office hours."

The first case was a young Marine who had been UA for twenty-eight days. Had he been away for more than thirty days he would have been considered a deserter, a far more serious offense. UA Marines aware of the deadline usually return before it. The atmosphere at "office hours" is always tense, the board members standing at attention, Colonel Tief sitting behind an oak desk. He begins with a rote recital of the Marine's rights under Article 31 of the Uniform Code of Military Justice. Then the hearing begins:

> TIEF: What's your story?
>
> MARINE: I had a lot of family problems. My father is sick.
>
> TIEF: Did you ever attempt to call the Marines?
>
> MARINE: Yes, sir. A few times. They refused to pass on my calls to an officer. I spent forty dollars on phone calls, so I stopped.
>
> TIEF: Who wouldn't pass on your calls?
>
> MARINE: The Duty NCO at the desk. He told me the captain was busy or was out.
>
> TIEF: You're full of shit. You can't tell me you tried to talk to someone and couldn't. Do you think you're talking to a child? This is the second time this has happened, isn't it?
>
> MARINE: No, sir. First time.

TIEF: What do you mean, first time? You were here in front of me before and I reduced you one rank, isn't that so?

MARINE: Oh, yes, sir.

TIEF: And you went UA in Hawaii before that, and once before too. Isn't that true?

MARINE: [Nodding affirmatively]

TIEF: Obviously that last punishment didn't leave an impression. Why did you come back?

MARINE: I thought maybe I could get a hardship discharge.

TIEF: Didn't you get your ass back after twenty-eight days because two more days and you would have been a deserter?

MARINE: [No answer]

TIEF: Summary court-martial. Dismissed.

When the man left the room, Tief shook his head in disgust. "That man speaks with a forked tongue," he muttered. Turning to the other officers, he said, "Get that man before the administrative board, and let's get him out of the Corps."

While there are other officers on the "office hours" board, it is the ranking officer, in this case Tief, who makes the decisions. In the case of another UA, Tief decided again that the man should be gotten out of the Corps. The third man before the board, UA for fifteen days because of family troubles and because his girl friend was pregnant, was ordered to see a chaplain, busted one grade, restricted to quarters for fifteen days, and ordered to forfeit twenty-five dollars in pay. The next man, a Puerto Rican from the Bronx, declared a deserter, was recommended for a summary court-martial. On a red armband worn to identify him as a maximum-security prisoner, the young Marine had printed "Viva PR" and on his sleeve cuff he had written with a ball-point pen, "Young Lords," the name of a group of Puerto Rican militants located in East Harlem.

Tief and McCoy, both experienced corrections officers, are rare persons in the Marine brig system, although the Corps states that it is moving ahead with a program to install professional correctional personnel throughout the Marine prison system. Until now, guards and other personnel have been ordinary Marines, most of them Vietnam veterans, a fact that creates considerable tension between them and confinees who, for the most part, are Marines who have gone UA to avoid Vietnam service. The seeds of brutality are deeply implanted in such a situation.

Allegations of such brutality were made openly by the Brooklyn brig prisoners interviewed, although Tief and McCoy denied knowledge of any such instances.

Unlike the brig interviews at Parris Island, which were attended by a bevy of Marine brass, the ones the authors conducted at the Brooklyn brig were strictly private. This marks the first time that the Marine Corps has ever permitted newsmen to talk to prisoners alone, a precedent that could have far-reaching implications not only for journalists but for the accused and their counsel.

One of the most frequent complaints of the inmates of the Brooklyn brig was about food, both quality and quantity:

> MARINE: They say they give us enough rations, but sometimes some of these guys do without because at the end of the chow line there isn't enough to go around. They only give out one piece of bread.
>
> AUTHORS: They tell us a man gets as much food as he wants except for meat portions.
>
> MARINE: What they tell you and what actually goes on is two different things. I think they're bullshitting you, pulling the wool over your eyes

to make it look good. Most of the people you talk to are career men. They believe in the Corps, they live the Corps, they die the Corps. It's this way: sometimes a guy's last in chow line, there's no potatoes, sometimes no meat. If the IG's [Inspectors General] come in, they sweat a little bit and they try to put out more food so the IG's won't believe the bitchin' they hear. The guy behind the line has to serve what the sergeant tells him to—one spoonful, one cookie, one cup of milk, one cup of coffee, one cup of tea. If you get two cups of anything, you got to sneak around and get it.

Others interviewed also complained about the lack of what they considered ample helpings of food at meals. They also criticized the quality of the food. One prisoner, nervously eyeing sentries and speaking in a whisper as the authors toured the mess hall, reported, "A guy just found ants in his saltine crackers. He wanted to talk to you, so he goes up to the sergeant, right, and says that he found ants in his crackers. So the sergeant says that the guy must be seeing things and takes away the crackers and throws them away."

Not all prisoners get the regular meals. Some, for reasons of punishment, are put on a disciplinary diet, an austere menu consisting mostly of starchy foods that fill a man's belly but hardly nourish him. Disciplinary diet for punishment in the Army may not exceed fourteen days. There is no time limit on the diet in the Marines. The only other disciplinary diet harsher than that authorized for use by the Marines is a bread-and-water diet, but it may be authorized only aboard ships of the Navy at sea. The disciplinary diet will provide a man about 2,100 calories a day on a menu similar to this:

BREAKFAST	QUANTITY	CALORIES
Dry cereal	¾ cup	70
Griddle cakes	2 slices	396
Hot toast	2 slices	140
DINNER		
Mashed potatoes	1½ cups	375
Harvard beets	2 cups	140
Assorted crisp relishes	1½ cups	55
Bread	2 slices	140
SUPPER		
American fried potatoes	1 cup	480
Buttered peas	1½ cups	228
Bread	2 slices	140
	TOTAL	2,164

One prisoner in the Brooklyn brig stated that he had been put on the disciplinary diet three times within five months. The first time was for fifty-seven days. The second, for fourteen days. The third, seven days.

A second inmate told Biaggi:

> MARINE: They give you cereal in the morning. No milk, no sugar. Just a regular box of cereal.
> BIAGGI: Do they give you water with it?
> MARINE: You drink the water out of the faucet. You get a box of corn flakes, you gotta eat 'em raw.

A third Marine:

> BIAGGI: Have you ever been on a disciplinary diet?
> MARINE: Yes, I was, for twenty or twenty-two days, somewhere around there.
> BIAGGI: Why were you put on that diet?
> MARINE: I couldn't do PT [physical training].

A sailor interviewed by Biaggi's aide, Dom Frasca:

> FRASCA: How long have you been on disciplinary diet?
> SAILOR: I been on it for two weeks, but I was on *restricted* diet for nine days.
> FRASCA: What does it consist of?
> SAILOR: Potatoes, two big spoonfuls of potatoes, and four pieces of bread.
> FRASCA: What do you have for breakfast?
> SAILOR: Potatoes. Same thing for breakfast, for dinner, for supper.
> FRASCA: What do you think of the diet?
> SAILOR: I don't like it. Nobody likes it.
> FRASCA: Do you feel weak?
> SAILOR: Yeah. I was hungry.

A twenty-nine-year-old Vietnam veteran who had been in the Marine Corps two and a half years was sent to St. Alban's Hospital for treatment of a liver disease. He threw down his tray in a mess hall and was sent to the brig. This was his second time on the disciplinary diet. His first time had been for four weeks.

> FRASCA: What's a typical meal like?
> MARINE: Four slices of bread, an orange, whole lot of potatoes, some lettuce.
> FRASCA: How did you feel on the diet?
> MARINE: The first time it bothered me. The second time I didn't eat for a solid week.

The Marine admitted that given his choice between this diet and the food in Vietnam, he would choose the disciplinary diet, not because it was better food but because "over there sometimes you don't get chow for a while" because of the combat situation.

Still another Marine who spent time in the Brooklyn brig for UA was given one week on the disciplinary diet as well as solitary confinement for attempting to escape. "It was about twenty-three hundred calories a day, all vegetables with no salt or flavoring. No meats or sweets and just water. Breakfast was potatoes or beans, enough to fill you up. Maybe some bread. Lunch and supper, about the same thing. Always the same thing."

Colonel Tief insisted that a man's case would be reviewed after ten days on the disciplinary diet. "That doesn't mean to say that a man goes on a diet ten days arbitrarily, but ten days is my upper limit for a real good, hard review. In the past we've gone for eighteen days. There is no ceiling in our regulations." Biaggi said Colonel Tief had advised him that the disciplinary diet was discontinued. However, prisoners were still on the diet during the authors' probe, three months later.

Harassment of brig prisoners is an integral part of the Brooklyn brig, as it is of all others, and a major technique for harassment is to require constant cleaning, mopping, dusting, and scrubbing. An embittered prisoner complained, "I can see mopping the floor in the morning or at night, but when you have to do it five or six times—! We dust. We dust thoroughly, and the sentry leaves the windows open so dust gets on the lockers. He comes around, checks it, makes us dust all over again. This goes on all the time."

And there are complaints about physical abuse.

A private who had been in the brig for five months told how he was beaten by three guards as he was being taken to disciplinary segregation.

"Do you have any other cases where sentries beat prisoners? he was asked.

"Well," he replied, "there was this prisoner named Stuart. Sergeants always beat him. Once they put handcuffs on him and raised his hands above his head and started smacking him in the face. At least four or five times a week the sentries would go in Stuart's cell and whip on him."

Another prisoner related how a sentry made men under his command stand at attention for a full day.

"Sometimes if a guard doesn't like you," said another inmate, "he'll ride you pretty hard. They try to push you into a fight so they can put you in segregation."

Going down a mental list of complaints in his interview, this Marine brought up the matter of cigarettes.

In the Brooklyn brig, a man is allowed an initial issue of three cartons of cigarettes and thereafter, out of the pay he collects while in the brig, he is permitted to buy three cartons of cigarettes a month at the exchange store on the first floor of the building. Warrant Officer McCoy pointed out that, although the exchange has a rule limiting customers to two cartons of cigarettes at a time, the prisoners are allowed to buy three because they go to the exchange only once a month.

But according to the prisoner who brought up the question of cigarettes, the choice of brands is limited. The initial issue of cigarettes, he said, is Raleigh or Bel Air. These brands give coupons which, the prisoner claimed, the guards confiscate. "They keep the coupons to pick up stuff for themselves to have," he claimed.

This same prisoner complained about the lack of recreational facilities. "All we do for exercise is PT," he said.

McCoy disputes this charge: "One detail goes to the gym on the first deck every night to play basketball," he stated. "Each person plays basketball at least twice if not three times a week."

Various types of prisoners are handled in various ways.

To distinguish between the types, the Brooklyn brig uses armbands. A red armband is a danger sign, symbol of a very difficult, and often dangerous, prisoner. These men are often put in segregation cells. Yellow armbands represent medium custody. "They're not good, they're not bad," explained McCoy. White armbands signify what in civilian prisons would be trustees, men who have progressed enough and have proved their reliability enough to be given certain privileges, such as TV and a job where they are not always supervised by guards. Green armbands would have been used to carry out the red-yellow-green color scheme of traffic lights, but no green material was available.

An efficient in-processing and screening program has been established. A man entering the brig will be processed within three hours. He'll be interviewed by a psychiatrist, a chaplain, and a counselor. He will be checked for scars and bruises and these will be noted, a precaution against brutality charges. Made to strip for this examination, the in-coming man will also have to submit to an examination to see if he has concealed drugs on his person. "Bend over and spread your cheeks," is the order. Within five days the brig officials know pretty well what kind of prisoner they have in their midst and they then assign him the appropriate confinement.

For those destined to a long stay in the brig, a general education program is available, supported by a reasonably good library, despite an allegation from one prisoner that the brig had no library facility. The educational program has made it possible, according to Colonel Tief, for some men to get high school diplomas.

"We have initiated a black studies program as an experiment," Tief said proudly, "which will probably continue. It is not just for blacks but for all those in the brig that are interested. It is taught by one of our lawyers. We think it's a pretty good course—strictly the history, customs, and culture of the black people. I don't know how much we'll expand this or where, but it's an experiment in the direction of trying to teach people and try to prepare them better to step back into society."

Tief admits to racial problems but feels he has the situation under control because he has excellent NCO's. He does say, however, that the racial problem has worsened during recent years because younger blacks are coming into the Marines, bringing with them the racial tensions of the streets.

In showing the authors the brig library, Tief admitted to a lack of Jewish Bibles. "The only one we have is in the chaplain's office, and he just got it. Anybody that requests that one, we send down to the chaplain and get it."

The authors asked if the brig would take a donation of a larger supply. Tief happily agreed. The Bibles have been provided by the Union of American Hebrew Congregations.

Throughout the tour of his facility and in the course of talking about his problems, Tief returned often to the brig's major problem—drugs.

"We just recently started a drug education program," he explained. "Every prisoner sees two drug movies a week. We show them in the dormitory by taking a screen and projector in there. We also show a full-length movie every Saturday."

This, obviously, is an officer with an enlightened and concerned approach to his duties as commander of the brig. He and Warrant Officer McCoy impressed the authors as men genuinely interested in the field of corrections. McCoy recently completed an American University program in that field. Each expected both prisoners and guards to toe the line, but, as in so many instances in the Corps, there appears to exist a large gap in communications between the lower echelons, where irregularities occur, and the upper echelons, where irregularities are condemned. Although some of the tales of abuse and maltreatment told by the inmates of the Brooklyn brig may have been embroidered for our benefit, there was obviously an underlying truth in them. It may be that these incidents did not reach the men at the top, Tief and McCoy, as some prisoners suggested. Both men demonstrated a real interest in the men confined to their brig. They were firm and not prepared to be misled, of course. Each seemed to have a good knowledge of special cases, especially the men considered suicide risks.

Near the end of the authors' visit to the Brooklyn brig, one of the guiding officers was handed what appeared to be a note. The officer read the note and passed it on to the authors. It appeared to be written in red crayon. It was barely legible.

"One of the men wants you to know his name, rank, and serial number," the officer said.

No one had to explain how desperate this prisoner was. The note had been scrawled in blood.

The prisoner, wanting desperately to talk, had battered his head against a wall, dipped a crumpled cigarette into his own blood, and scrawled the note. The boy was deeply depressed and had tried suicide on several occasions, once trying to drown himself by immersing his head in a commode. He was depressed when he found out he was not going to be sent back to Camp Lejeune.

"Well, I'll tell you, young man, you were set to leave here up until you did that," said McCoy with some irritation and disappointment in his voice. "But when you did that we *couldn't* put you on a bus and send you back. Now, *if* you behave, you can probably leave this Wednesday."

The prisoner said he wanted his bunk back.

The bunk had been removed as a precaution against suicide. This man had slashed himself by using part of his bunk. Men devise ingenious ways of using parts of bunks to attempt to slash their wrists or bludgeon themselves, and suicide risks are usually denied bunks. This prisoner would be denied one again, until the officials felt more certain about him.

Some men in the brig are probably well beyond any help from McCoy and Tief. Deeply embittered by the experience of the Vietnam war, some have given up entirely and lapsed into a frame of mind that is defeatist and depressing. One of these men landed in a brig in Vietnam because he absented himself from his unit when it was scheduled to go into combat. Asked if he had been scared, he replied:

> I was scared from the first day I got over there until the day I left. They say when you're over there that you're "salty," but that's not true. When I first went over to 'Nam, I thought it was cowboys-and-Indians until I seen my buddies die, until I got hit with an AK-47, a Chinese semi-automatic rifle. Then I began to realize this was no place for Americans to be, because we got our own problems right back here in the States. When I first come in the Marines I was thinking of making a career in the Corps. Now that I'm in I know that you're not a man in the Marines, you're just a number or a machine. They say that in 'Nam you're fighting for your country. Not me. When I was over there, I was fighting for my life. That's the *only* thing I was fighting for.

Desperation such as that is found in abundance in the Brooklyn brig—indeed, in all brigs.

We witnessed, briefly, another kind of desperation.

When we entered the brig at the start of the tour, written in grease pencil on a board used to log the names of newly arrived prisoners was a single, intriguing word: DEFECTOR.

"Can you tell us about the defector?" we asked.

"We don't even know the full story," said Warrant Officer McCoy, "and we can't give it to you. We can't let you. . . .

He hasn't been interrogated yet. So we don't know what he'll tell you. We won't even ask him."

"Where was he brought in from?" we asked.

"I don't even know this," McCoy said. He tried to laugh. "This is how much I know about it."

By the time we returned to the location where the board with its intriguing word had caught our attention, the word had been erased.

Not for the first time, the Marine Corps had preceded us with a kind of alarm about our impending arrival. At Parris Island, every low-echelon commander had been alerted to our expected tour of that facility. Colonel Tief, when called by us to make the initial arrangements for the visit to the Brooklyn brig, knew before we even told him what we wanted to see. Word of our research for this book reached the Marine recruiters in New York but not, fortunately, before we had already conducted those interviews. If not exactly pleased at the prospect of being regarded as a cause for alarm throughout the Corps, we found that the Marine communications system was effective and impressive. But we also found that the Marines, reconciling themselves to the fact that a book was going to be published about them, threw up surprisingly few stumbling blocks. We like to think that this was a gesture of acknowledgment of our tenacity as reporters, but we also admit that the Corps did not always try, as a brig inmate suggested, to bullshit us.

At the Brooklyn brig we saw what we wanted to see, talked to those we wanted to talk to, and got straight answers, for the most part, from the high command.

We did not get to see the elusive "defector," but we doubt that he could possibly have been as spectacular as a previous Marine defector, one Corporal Rafael Minichiello, the most daring and imaginative Marine ever to hijack an airliner.

CHAPTER ELEVEN

JUSTICE, MARINE-STYLE

With respect to the rights that a service-man enjoys, we have been far, far ahead of the civilian courts for years.
Brigadier General Duane L. Faw

Like most Marines, Lance Corporal Rafael Minichiello liked beer. He also liked motorcycle magazines and paperback novels. He was always ready to go to a base movie with fellows from his barracks at Camp Pendleton. He liked flying, was taking lessons, and had graduated from parachutists' school. A small, quiet, black-haired, Italian-born boy, he had a lot of friends in the Marines with whom he swapped stories about war experiences in Vietnam, where he'd won a medal for gallantry.

Soon after his return from the war, Minichiello told one of his buddies, Corporal Bruce S. Greeler of Minneapolis, Minnesota, that the Marine Corps had cheated him out of some money. The young Marine felt that he had been cheated of two hundred dollars he'd left on deposit while in Vietnam. Instead of getting the eight hundred dollars that he had calculated was rightfully his in unpaid salary, he received only six hundred. Greeler said the boy was very angry, and "When Minichiello gets mad, he really gets mad."

To get his money back, Minichiello broke into a PX, taking what he figured was the money's equivalent in merchandise. Arrested on May 17, 1969, by San Diego police and charged with housebreaking and larceny, Minichiello was held at the city jail until the Marines took over the case. Civilian charges were dropped and Minichiello was ordered to stand trial in military court for his offenses. If convicted, he would have to face up to six months in prison and a bad conduct discharge.

"He seemed scared," Greeler said, adding, "I'd be scared, too."

Prior to his court-martial, Minichiello was performing janitorial services at Camp Pendleton and brooding about the possibility of being confined to the infamous Pendleton brig. On the day of his scheduled court-martial, Minichiello was nowhere around. Minichiello had gone to Los Angeles, boarded a T.W.A. plane heading east, and hijacked the airliner.

He made no indication of his ultimate destination, so for hours the world was fascinated by the reports that came in over radio and television of the boldness and the daring of the exploit, an in-air adventure that spanned two continents and an ocean as the Italian-born Minichiello, armed with a rifle, forced the plane to fly from Denver, where he permitted passengers to disembark, to Kennedy airport in New York, where FBI agents attempted to apprehend him but bungled the job, to Bangor, Maine, for refueling, to Shannon, Ireland, for more fuel, and at last to Rome, Italy. Minichiello's run for freedom ended after a brief escape from authorities at the Rome airport. The youth was taken into custody meekly inside a rural church. Reunited with his father, standing on the soil of his native land, a hero of sorts to the Italian people, Rafael Minichiello had thwarted the wheels of justice of the U.S. Marines by fleeing to a country that would insist on trying him for local violations rather than extraditing him back to California. Critics of the U.S. military courts system found in the Minichiello case another opportunity to attack the court-martial system.

"The words military and justice," they said, "are contradictory."

These critics maintain that the only purpose of military courts is to debase a man or to destroy his life and reputation.

All persons serving in the armed forces of the United States are subject to the Military Justice Act of 1968, effective August 1, 1969. This law is basically the same code that has governed the military for decades, but with some reforms and changes. It modified the Uniform Code of Military Justice, 1950.

A code of laws for the governing of the military has existed in one form or another in the United States since the earliest days of the Revolution. The Continental Congress adopted military and naval articles in 1775. The Articles of War for the new American Army were copied from the 1765 British Articles of War and were in effect for a year, until they were redrafted by John Adams. Revisions were made again in 1806, 1874, 1916, and 1948. That year was a high point of criticism of the court-martial system. A long process of review and revision was undertaken. On May 31, 1951, there became effective Public Law 81-506, the Uniform Code of Military Justice. The revisions in 1969 updated and changed other aspects of the basic Code, and it is the 1969 version of the code that now governs the millions of men and women who wear the uniforms of the armed services of the United States.

The code is again under attack from critics who claim that it violates the basic rights of citizenship granted to all Americans under the Constitution, contentions that reflect a less than thorough knowledge of the provisions of our founding charter, which states that not all civil rights are intended to apply to persons in military service.

"Of the protections enumerated in the Bill of Rights, the right to a trial only upon the presentment and indictment of a grand jury is expressly denied to servicemen in the Fifth Amendment," points out Robert M. Ujevich, legislative attorney, American Law Division, the Library of Congress, in the library's 1960 report, *Military Justice: A Summary of Its Legislative and Judicial Development.* Ujevich further writes:

> Additionally, those protections enumerated in the Second, Third, Seventh, Ninth, and Tenth Amendments do not appear to be relevant to the military. The remaining protections, though apparently applicable, are nevertheless classifiable as inappropriate, unknown to military law, or incapable of full enjoyment by the military. Whether the Founding Fathers intended this consequence in the application of these protections to courts-martial proceedings is a subject that has been treated to a scholarly but inconclusive debate in the legal journals, and comprehensive but conflicting treatment and results in the appropriate courts. And regardless of the ultimate outcome of this debate on the academic level, it remains, for the present at least, that the dominant principle in the federal courts is that persons subject to courts-martial possess only those rights (Constitutional or otherwise) granted them by Congress.

The rights of service personnel depend wholly on Acts

of Congress and decisions of the Court of Military Appeals, the armed services' equivalent of the Supreme Court of the United States.

In short, when a man or woman raises a hand to take the oath on entering military service, the basic Constitutional rights enjoyed as civilians are waived. The person entering the service becomes subject to a quite different set of rights, protections, and laws—the Uniform Code of Military Justice.

The code establishes a military court system. Articles 16 through 21 identify these courts-martial and specify their jurisdiction and number of members of each.

There are three kinds of military court—special, summary, and general.

A special court-martial consists of not less than three members, or a military judge and not less than three members. Its jurisdiction is generally limited to the trial of noncapital offenses, although capital offenses may be tried when specified by the President of the United States. Specifically banned are judgments of death, dishonorable discharge, dismissal, confinement for more than six months, hard labor without confinement for more than three months, forfeiture of pay exceeding two-thirds pay per month, or forfeiture of pay for more than six months. Under some conditions a bad-conduct discharge may be awarded.

A summary court-martial consists of one commissioned officer. It handles noncapital offenses. Punishments forbidden in summary courts are death, dismissal, dishonorable or bad conduct discharge, confinement of more than a month, hard labor without confinement for more than forty-five days, restriction to certain specified limits for more than two months, or forfeiture of more than two-thirds of one month's pay.

A general court-martial consists of a military judge and not less than five members, or only a military judge if special prerequisites are met. It handles offenses covered by the rules of war. Cruel and unusual punishments are forbidden.

Offenses under the Uniform Code of Military Justice may also be handled under another provision, NJP (non-judicial punishment), known in all the Armed Forces as Article 15. This article of the UCMJ provides a means whereby military commanders may deal with minor infractions of military discipline without resort to the criminal law process. Punishments under Article 15 generally include extra duties, withholding of privileges, and restriction to specified areas. None of these punishments may exceed two weeks.

Action taken under Article 15 is not considered as a conviction of a crime and technically has no connection with the military court system. It is by far the most widely used method for imposing punishments.

Of these cases that actually go to courts-martial, few reach the ultimate end of the court-martial system, the Court of Military Appeals. Critics of the UCMJ state that in 1968 there were 89,649 courts-martial of all kinds in all services and that of these only 121 were accepted by the Court of Military Appeals. That amounts to 0.13 per cent of all cases. This seems an appallingly small number, but the statistics on the number of cases in American civil courts that actually reach and are adjudicated by the Supreme Court of the United States are scarcely overwhelming. There may be sound arguments against many aspects of the courts-martial system, but the inference that every court-martial case should be reviewed by the military's highest court is like asking the U.S. Supreme Court to review all cases tried in all of the nation's courts.

In calendar year 1968, in which the above 89,649 courts-martial were held, the United States Marine Corps held 9,313. Of these, 410 were general, 5,282 were special, and 3,621 were summary: 5,564 were held at West Coast Marine facilities, and 3,749 were at East Coast ones. The Marines explain that the West Coast figures are higher because it is "the mouth of the funnel through which all Marines being transferred to the west Pacific flow."

In 1968 the Marines gave bad-conduct discharges to 593 men on the West Coast through special courts-martial, and 487 BCD's were given as punishment on the East Coast. In that year, Parris Island held 16 general courts-martial, 260 special courts-martial (36 of them BCD), and 215 summary courts-martial.

The Judge Advocate General of the Navy, Rear Admiral Joseph B. McDevitt, provided further statistics on the activities of military courts in the Navy (including Marines) in 1968: "It is pointed out that there were 29,337 court-martial trials in the Naval service during calendar year 1968 and that 43,952 offenses were involved in those trials [one trial often includes more than one offense]."

Admiral McDevitt reported that an estimated "less than 3 per cent of all court-martial offenses committed by Navy and Marine Corps personnel have been civil-type offenses committed in the civilian community. Thus, approximately 97 per cent of all offenses are committed on board Naval ships and installations." Of the 43,952 court-martial offenses committed by Navy personnel in 1968, 42,633 were committed on board Naval ships and installations. Two-thirds were UA cases.

These figures seem to bear out the opinion of Senator Sam Ervin, chairman of the Constitutional Rights Subcommittee of the Senate Judiciary Committee, that "the primary purpose of the administration of justice in the military services is to enforce discipline, plus getting rid of people who think they are not capable of contributing to the defense of the country as they should."

That the military courts system is used as an enforcer of discipline is the basis for criticism of the military justice system where, it is alleged, a man may enter the courts only as a defendant and never as a plaintiff.

One of the critics of the system is New York Congressman Hugh L. Carey: "The time has come for a close look into the legal rights of servicemen and the military penal system."

"With respect to the rights that a serviceman enjoys, we have been far, far ahead of the civilians for years," says Brigadier General Duane L. Faw, head of the Judge Advocate General Division, USMC. "In the first place, a man is guaranteed a lawyer. Right now, we can't give a man any kind of punitive discharge without giving him a lawyer. He must be defended by a lawyer. Since 1951 he not only has had the right to be defended by a lawyer, he *must* be defended by a lawyer."

Critics maintain that this is a sham. They allege that in any court-martial where the pride of the brass is at stake, or where the brass feels the need to make an example of the defendant, the defense attorney is at an extreme disadvantage.

This same charge has been made by a civilian attorney who defended the Green Berets when they were charged with murdering a Vietnamese double agent, a case that was ultimately dropped by the Army because it could not proceed without the assistance of the Central Intelligence Agency, which refused to allow its agents to testify. Attorney Henry B. Rothblatt maintained in an article he wrote for *True* magazine that of all the "faults" in the Uniform Code of Military Justice, the "most insidious" is command influence. Rothblatt said in the article that as long as a commanding officer had no interest in the proceedings, the UCMJ was "probably fair." But if a commander's ego was involved, Rothblatt charged, if the commander knew he had something at stake personally, if for some reason "personal antipathy toward the accused" was involved, then the commander's influence would pervade the proceedings.

Rothblatt concluded with an appeal for changes in the UCMJ that would eliminate the possibility of command influence in the conduct of trials for military personnel. Calling the matter of command influence a "menace" that made a mockery of the whole concept of military justice under the existing code, attorney Rothblatt insisted that this was a situation that must be changed if soldiers at the front and elsewhere were to get a fair shake in the military courts.

General Faw comments on the possibility that accused men would not get a fair trial under the UCMJ. He believes that the military court-martial system has built-in protections in the form of higher reviews of all cases.

Faw states that Marines or other servicemen brought up on charges and tried are guaranteed reviews of their cases:

> We automatically require that the accused man be provided with a verbatim transcript of the record if he receives a punitive discharge. The record is automatically reviewed at two higher levels after the trial. No civilian has ever had this. The case then goes to a third review board, the Navy Board of Review, so an individual tried by a special court-martial is actually reviewed at three levels. At every one of these levels everybody has the right to disapprove the lower findings, to reduce those findings to a lesser sentence, or to disapprove or suspend the sentence. They can never be increased in any way. A man then has the opportunity and right to appeal to the Court of Military Appeals, our highest court.

General Faw pointed out that in civilian courts appeals were just that, appeals. "Someone must complain," he said.

> In the Marines, this is an *automatic* review. In civilian courts, the defendant would have to express to the higher court a reason why the case should be considered at a

higher level. In military law, everyone goes before them, up to the level of the Court of Military Appeals. At that level, the Court of Military Appeals will not review the case unless somebody complains. Then those complaining have to make their case, just as they do to get a case before the United States Supreme Court, but even then, in these appeals to the military's highèst court, a lawyer is furnished free of charge.

Military personnel may have civilian lawyers, but General Faw believes, after his experience with civilian lawyers in military courts, that a serviceman gets a better deal if he uses military lawyers, who are familiar with the subtleties of the court-martial system. Faw believes that one of the mistakes a civilian lawyer will make is to insist on having enlisted men, rather than officers, in the majority on a general court-martial.

Under the military code, any defendant may request enlisted personnel on the court-martial. In such requests, the panel must include enlisted men, and by judicious use of peremptory challenges, an astute defense lawyer can arrange the court panel so that enlisted men are in the majority. Faw says he experimented with enlisted men on courts-martial when he was a defense lawyer and regretted the experiment. "These are the guys who are behaving themselves, and they expect all enlisted personnel to do the same." Courts with enlisted men tend to be more severe in punishing.

The U.S. Marines say they dislike giving men less than honorable discharges. A 1963 order from the Commandant said these discharges "must be reduced," and even today the Marines are greatly concerned about the conditions of discharge under which its men leave the ranks of the Corps. Yet this desire to have men separated only under the best possible conditions leaves the Corps on the horns of a dilemma, because the Corps recognizes that it has within its ranks some men who do not belong in the Marines, who should never have been admitted initially, and who are nothing but headaches. The Corps has recently devised a program it calls "operation clean house." This program is designed to discharge undesirable Marines for administrative reasons before they find themselves in situations that might lead to less than honorable circumstances of separation.

"Men such as these have basic problems," General Faw believes, "psychological disturbances, personality behaviors, inabilities physically or emotionally to conform to the standards of the military. Of these, many are the result of sick parents. Sick parents get their boys in trouble more than many people realize—immature kid, mother-oriented. The history of the Corps is replete with sons who have spent time in the brig for the sins of their parents. 'Operation clean house' will deal with this sort of unfortunate boy without the terrible punishment of something like a BCD."

Advised of the words of a prisoner in the Parris Island brig who felt that a bad conduct discharge was something that could be overcome in civilian life, General Faw shook his head, tugged at his lower lip, and signed deeply. "That just isn't the case," he said. "A BCD is a terrible punishment," he repeated.

In the files of Marine headquarters in Washington are letters from men discharged under less than honorable conditions. They are ample testimony to the severity of punishment that includes separation under these conditions.

"In so much as I have paid the penalty for my mistake, that I so greatly regret, and have an opportunity for a position which I qualify for and may never have this opportunity again, I am asking to have my bad conduct discharge changed to a general discharge so I will not have to go through life without a job I qualify for, due to this BCD," wrote one ex-Marine.

The inability to get satisfactory employment or to advance in one's job is the most frequent result of a BCD. "It always comes up in my jobs," another BCD Marine wrote to the Marine headquarters.

The letters that come in can be touching:

> This statement is primarily in behalf of my wife and four children. In these trying years, it is hard enough to provide a living for your family with a "good" discharge. For me it is practically impossible. Why must my family be punished for eternity for mistakes that I made, even before they existed? If I am to be punished for the rest of my life, why not do it some other way?

Men serving in the brig and awaiting final disposition of their cases also write to the Marine headquarters to plead against a BCD. "I don't want a BCD because I feel it would make my life and my family's life a lot harder than it has been. I couldn't look my friends in the eye and say that I got a BCD," wrote a Marine from the Parris Island brig.

Similar appeals come to the Corps for remission of discharges under less than honorable conditions, most of them because these discharges have a powerful effect on the ability of these men to find employment in civilian life, largely because civilians have come to expect that men who fail to meet the test of the Marine Corps (and other armed services) cannot measure up as civilians.

Whether the current, growing mistrust of the military will lead the general population to revise its standards for judging the conditions of a man's discharge remains to be seen, but there does not appear to be any movement among the great majority of Americans to take a more tolerant attitude toward men who have washed out of the military, especially out of the Marines. If there is movement, it is probably toward an even more severe condemnation of these men.

The Corps looks on discharges under less than honorable conditions as an admission that the Corps has failed, and because the Corps feels that it has been made to admit failure, there remains forever a resentment against the men who have brought discredit in this way to themselves and to the Corps. Letters appealing for changes in less than honorable discharges are largely answered negatively. The 1963 Marine Corps order dealing with less than honorable discharges warned Marines that conditions of a discharge are not easily changed. Stating that there was widespread feeling that "an unfavorable-type discharge can be easily recharacterized after discharge, through the simple means of petitioning the Navy Discharge Review Board," the Marine Commandant stated flatly, "This is not the case." He pointed out that only 12.03 per cent of the petitions received the previous year had been favorably acted on by the Navy Discharge Review Board.

In 1963 one of the petitioners declined by the board was an ex-Marine named Lee Harvey Oswald.

In many ways, according to testimony given by Oswald's Marine colleagues to the President's Commission on the Assassination of President John F. Kennedy, Oswald was a classic case of a recalcitrant Marine destined to get into trouble in the Corps. He was court-martialed on two occasions and had a record of baiting and talking back to officers and noncoms. "While there is nothing in Oswald's military records to indicate that he was mentally unstable or otherwise psychologically unfit for duty in the Marine Corps," stated the Warren Commission Report, "he did not adjust well to conditions which he found in that service.

He did not rise above the rank of Private First Class, even though he had passed a qualifying examination for the rank of Corporal. His Marine career was not helped by his attitude that he was a man of great ability and intelligence and that many of his superiors in the Marine Corps were not sufficiently competent to give him orders."

In the Marines, Oswald seemed to John E. Donovan, one of his former officers, to be a young man who thought the Marines had failed to recognize his talent. Another Marine, Kerry Thornley, saw in Oswald a "recalcitrant trend."

Another Marine who knew Oswald well was Allen D. Graf, who had been Oswald's platoon sergeant in California. He told the Warren Commission:

> Oswald often complained about the Marine Corps; he seemed to me to resent all military authority. He also seemed narrow-minded, refusing to listen to the views of others.
>
> Once, at the rifle range, I had a long discussion with Oswald concerning why he found it difficult to adapt to the Marine Corps. He explained that his mother had had a great deal of trouble during the Depression and that when he was young, he had often not had enough to eat. He felt that he had been forced to accept responsibility at a premature age. He remarked that he was tired of being "kicked around."

On his own request, Oswald was transferred from the active to the reserve Marines because his mother had been injured in an accident. Later, when Oswald defected to the Soviet Union, he was given an undesirable discharge, which he sought to have changed by appealing directly to Secretary of the Navy John Connally. He wrote on January 30, 1962, that he would "employ all means to right this gross mistake or injustice."

"It is clear that he thought he had been unjustly treated," concluded the Warren Report.

The Navy Review Board, which had rejected nine out of ten men asking for modifications of their discharges in 1962, turned Oswald down, too, on July 25, 1963.

There are students of the Oswald affair who believe that the fatal shots fired in Dallas on November 22, 1963, were aimed not at President John F. Kennedy or former Navy Secretary Connally but at that undesirable discharge from the Marines. The Warren Commission stated that "to the extent Oswald's undesirable discharge affected his motivation, it was more in terms of a general hostility against the government and its representatives rather than a grudge against any particular person."

Lee Harvey Oswald and Rafael Minichiello were not the first Marines to bridle against its customs, traditions, and requirements and to feel that they had been unjustly handled by the Corps. These two men happened to become notorious by their personal, private acts, but because they were Marines there must always linger the question how much their ultimate personal acts of rebellion against authority through criminal acts were shaped by the constant atmosphere of violence that pervades the Corps.

"The Marine Corps is not an isolated segment of American life," said psychologist Waldo Lyon.

The Marines know this and are extremely sensitive at the highest levels of Command to public criticism. This is never more true than in cases of criticism of the Marine judicial system. The Corps will state confidently that the purpose of its judicial system is not to punish but to reform, to rehabilitate, to make an errant individual into a Marine. Nonetheless, the Marine system of justice is as much a part of the Marine system of instilling discipline as boot-camp hazing. "On the other side of the coin from military discipline," said Lieutenant General Lewis Walt, Assistant Commandant of the Corps, "is military justice."

CHAPTER TWELVE

"SEMPER FIDELIS"

This is a tough business.
    General Leonard F. Chapman, Jr.
    Commandant, USMC

On November 10, 1775, the Continental Congress meeting in Philadelphia ordered the creation of a Marine Corps as part of an American fleet the Congress was hastily putting together for the coming war with England. "The beat of history began at Philadelphia in 1775, at an impromptu recruiting station called Tun Tavern," says a Marine brochure. "The first Marines thought America had something worth fighting for. We still do."

The story is told of the first Marine to sign on with Lieutenant John Paul Jones aboard the *Alfred*. The new Marine was aboard about an hour when a second Marine signed on. "Hell, lad, you should have been in the *old* Corps," the original Marine said.

Out of those days in the beginning of what was to become the American nation grew the United States Marine Corps, an elite force of men who have been "the first to fight" in every American war since 1775. Since that day in 1775 when Captain Samuel Nicholas, the first Marine officer, opened his recruiting drive at Tun Tavern, millions of American men have worn the anchor-and-globe emblem of the Corps, and they have inscribed their own heroism and the "glory of the Corps" on the soil of places named Iwo Jima, Tarawa, Guadalcanal, Maui Peak, Henderson Hill, Garrard Bay, Porkchop Hill, Cuba, Belleau Wood, New Britain, New Georgia, Nouméa, and a thousand places between.

"In the beginning the purpose of our armed forces was the defense of this country," said Marine Corps Commandant Chapman at a luncheon of the New York Union League on January 22, 1970. "And then, as now, it required ships and weapons, and the equipage of war. But more important, it required people. Not just people in numbers, but individual men joined together in a spirit of dedication to duty and service. That we are here now, as Americans, counting our history in centuries, is proof that such men did serve—that such a spirit did exist. These men of dedication found service a simple matter. They believed in the people they served—the American public—and the people they served believed in them."

Leonard F. Chapman, Jr., became Commandant of the United States Marine Corps on January 1, 1968, succeeding General Wallace M. Greene, Jr.

Lean, tanned, fit, and square-jawed, Chapman is the kind of man one expects to be the commander of a military organization such as the Marines. He has served in the Corps since 1935, joining its ranks as a second lieutenant after graduation from the University of Florida. He was born November 3, 1913, in Key West, Florida. Aboard the U.S.S. *Astoria* when World War II broke out, Chapman took part in early raids in the Pacific and in the battles of Coral Sea and Midway, where he earned the Navy Commendation Ribbon as commander of a Marine detachment. During combat at Peleliu and Okinawa he earned the

Legion of Merit and the Bronze Star. After the war, he rose steadily through the commissioned ranks and in 1953 commanded the 12th Marines, 3d Marine Division. From 1956 to 1958 he commanded the Marine Barracks in Washington, D.C. Upon promotion to brigadier general in 1958 he was assigned as Commanding General, Force Troops, Fleet Marine Force, Atlantic. He became Chief of Staff, Marine Headquarters, in 1964 and Assistant Commandant on July 1, 1967, moving up one year later to the office of Commandant on the recommendation of President Johnson. Both his sons are Marine officers.

Chapman's entire life may be summed up in his words, spoken at a hearing of the House Armed Services Committee: "I am proud to represent the Marine Corps before you."

He is always ready to defend his Corps, although he believes the Corps needs no defense. He is also ready to attack elements in America that he feels are both alien to the American system and the enemies of it.

"At this point in time," he said in the Union League speech, "we face a multitude of problems that have generated shrill accusations and harsh demands. And in the midst of all these internal problems we are at war. We have, for the past five years, been engaged in a hard, bitter conflict. It is, and I quote from the American news media, an "unpopular" war. Has any war ever really been popular? Did the men who fought at Bastogne and Iwo Jima actually enjoy World War II? Did the American fighting men on both sides in the Civil War find that agony and sacrifice popular? Of course not. Men who must bear the burden of combat, who must face possible death, never find war popular. But those other Americans of other wars did feel the support of their people. They did know their service was not in vain."

Throughout the commissioned ranks and among Marines NCO's there is a pervasive feeling that the country is letting down its armed services. This was reflected in our numerous conversations with enlisted men, DI's, officers, and the Marine high command. It could be a major morale problem in the Corps.

Confronting growing pacifism, isolationism, and anti-militarism plus the prospects for cutting back military spending, Chapman said:

> I would be less than truthful if I said that I was dis-appointed in these plans as far as the Marines are concerned. It is true that the cutbacks have curtailed Marine Corps mobility somewhat . . . [but] other than that we are not too concerned about the overall effect on the Corps. Marines like their Corps small, efficient, eco-nomical, and *certainly* all-volunteer. So as a Marine I agree in principle. But there is a danger creeping on this theory—these plans. That danger is the erosion of the spirit of service.

Chapman believes that plans to increase salaries and benefits as the draft is phased out are fine. "But you can't buy dedication," he says. He insists there must be a spirit of service.

"This is a tough business. No matter from what angle you're looking, it's hard, demanding life," he stated. "What I fear is the isolation of the armed forces from the rest of the country. The establishment of a separate philosophy. That is the real danger."

Chapman's feelings are echoed by others on his Marine headquarters staff.

One of those who puts the dilemma more bluntly is the number-two man in the Marines, Assistant Commandant Lewis Walt. Combat veteran, medal-winner, and basically a commander of troops in the field, Walt is a large man with massive shoulders and ice-blue eyes. "I know this," he told an interviewer. "If I were a private first class, or the parent or brother or sweetheart of one, and we were going into battle, I'd like to know that the men beside me were not only self-disciplined but members of a team. If they are, we might all survive. If they are not, if they have placed dissent above duty, then I think the chances are pretty good we will all die. Isn't that more of a price than the majority should pay for the dissent of the few?"

Dissent erodes discipline, and when discipline goes, men die needlessly.

This is the fundamental creed of the United States Marines. It has always been the creed. The individual must be subservient to the team, the squad, the platoon.

Walt and Chapman are not only talking about political dissent. They refer, too, to the man who rebels, who strikes back at the authority of the DI or other noncom or officer, the recalcitrant recruit in boot camp.

General O. F. Peatross, commander of Parris Island, who deals directly with the rawest of Marines—recruits— says the whole philosophy of the arduous training techniques used by the Corps is to expose a man's character, to see whether or not he can perform in combat. If that exposure shows the man is defective, the Corps feels it has the duty to remold him. Peatross makes no bones about the training being tough, but he also believes that there has been much exaggeration on the part of those who have gone through it.

"I know they exaggerate," he said. "For example, we have an athletic field here at Parris Island that we use once a month for a competition in chin-ups. The best man that does chin-ups does about twenty-one, twenty-two, or twenty-three. Occasionally you see someone do a few more. But I get letters and I read articles in newspapers saying that a man has to do fifty. We've never had a man do that. I read a newspaper article that quoted a Marine as saying he had to climb a fifty-foot rope. We don't have a vertical rope on this base higher than twenty-five feet. You can find a lot of Marines who say, 'When I went through recruit training I shot expert and I did this and that.' We know how many men shoot expert and we can tell you that a lot say they did when they didn't. We had a letter about two weeks ago about a recruit who claimed he had to do two thousand squat thrusts. I know of no record of any Marine that had to do one-tenth of that. It's fantastic to me the way it's exaggerated."

Maltreatment and brutality at Parris Island? No one will say they are unheard of, but Marine officials will insist that these are "isolated" cases, aberrations, or recruit exaggerations.

The fact is, maltreatment *does* exist, *is* condoned, and is *widely practiced.* Any Marine officer who maintains otherwise is either lying, ill-informed, or blind.

"Those Marine officers who survive the selection procedures to rise to high office are cosmopolitan, knowledgeable leaders," contends psychologist Waldo Lyon, himself a former Naval officer. "They truly believe that the Marine Corps has something positive to offer each youth. Idealistically, they feel that even those who fail have been 'helped' in some way. And the truth is that many youths learn that they can meet challenges and accomplish tasks beyond their expectations."

Brigadier General W. B. McKean, author of *Ribbon Creek,* a book dealing with the McKeon "death march," stated, "Marines are no damn good in peacetime. While they're in the field we want them to be tough, callous to human suffering, willing to hazard risks, phlegmatic about death. When they're home we want them to be proper gentlemen, considerate of their fellow man, adherent to rules of safety, striving for longevity. This double standard is certain to generate conflicts in the individual."

Conflicts may arise in individual Marines in wartime,

also. In Vietnam, in late February, 1970, five Marines on patrol about twenty-seven miles south of Da Nang allegedly stormed into hamlet No. 4 of Son Thang village and went on a murderous rampage, killing sixteen Vietnamese civilians in what appeared to be a gruesome replay of another alleged massacre in the village of My Lai, sixty miles northwest of Son Thang, in 1968.

"This location has been the scene of almost continuous sniper fire and booby trap casualties since Marines commenced operating there," explained Marine headquarters in Da Nang. The men were part of the 1st Marine Division, which was operating in the area and making regular patrols to flush out Viet Cong and North Vietnamese forces in the low, rocky hillocks in the Que Son Valley, an expanse of rice paddies, hedgerows, and treelines.

That such incidents occur should be no surprise. J. G. Gray, in *The Warriors,* wrote, "We would be appalled at the sinister and brutal forces our country can spawn overnight. Every nation, I believe, conceals in itself violent criminal forces, waiting only for an opportunity to appear in daylight." To that, Waldo Lyon adds, "Reports of isolated acts of viciousness in Vietnam by small groups of Marines suggest that these Marines collectively decided it was all right to torture and kill Vietnamese civilians."

Lyon, whose paper on his reflections after years of psychological evaluation of Marine Corps recruits put a spotlight on the brutalities of recruit life, was aware that the Marines would dispute him. "It seems likely that if these present remarks receive any wider notice," he said when delivering the paper to colleagues, "they will call forth the defense of denial—that such things don't really happen, or if they do, they are isolated instances. It is indeed difficult to accept the monstrous truth that maltreatment is a way of life of Marine training. We tend to condone these incidents as we defend ourselves against acknowledgment of our own dark side. Chaplains—men of God—fire the rifle and back up Drill Instructors because it is too intolerable to believe the tales told in the privacy of the chaplain's office."

The Marine Corps has established a policy on dissent and dissenters, which are an increasing internal problem for the Corps. For example, the Marines have been aware of a group calling itself Movement for a Democratic Military (MDM), a group that early in 1970 listed only fifty members but which got perhaps undue publicity because of a comment upon the group by General Chapman. In Los Angeles the Commandant said the Corps would keep pressure on these militant dissidents. He revealed that shore patrolmen in the San Diego area were checking cars near the MDM offices and noting those with military base stickers. "I don't think the MDM is a threat to our country or to the military at present," said Chapman, "but some of their objectives would be a threat if they became a reality. We are keeping an eye on those who frequent that office, because if they are members of the armed forces —be they Marines, sailors or soldiers—they will be dealt with to the full extent of military law."

The MDM said its objective was "to improve many areas of life in the service that we can't change through the chain of command."

MDM had earlier taken part in a noisy demonstration at Oceanside, California, in which Marine guards scuffled with them on the perimeter of Camp Pendleton. There were some Marines on the side of the MDM demonstrators during the melee.

On the subject of political dissenters within the ranks, General Walt said, "Such men are violating the oaths they have taken and, more seriously, they are endangering the security and welfare of their nation. They are involved in a dangerous, self-destructive process. Few if any great nations have fallen to enemies from without. They fall because of dissension within."

What Walt and other Marines ask is, "Give me a chance —give the Marine Corps a chance—with these misguided kids, and we'll change them. We'll give them a purpose in life, and that's what they lack."

There is no available evidence that dissent within the Marines is a vast conspiracy. Army Brigadier General Leo A. Benade, Deputy Assistant Secretary of Defense, wrote, "The protesters and dissident elements among servicemen represent a small fraction of the total number of men in uniform. Indications are that no more than 1 per cent of our servicemen involve themselves in dissident-type activities, and when dissent is expressed in an unlawful manner, appropriate action is taken against the individuals concerned."

The Marines do not feel they now have a problem with dissenters, but they are aware of the potential problem and say they are keeping their eye on it.

The Marines are also aware of their public-relations problem. Disclosures of cases of maltreatment in training have made the Corps "perhaps overly defensive," as Captain M. R. Arnold, the Parris Island public information officer, admitted to the authors, but the Marines are also confident that they can handle their "image" problem.

Public-relations programs have been instituted with proper public fanfare to take the edge off criticisms leveled at the Corps.

One of these is the Youth Physical Fitness Program. This program of physical education has the support of the Commandant of the Corps and is run through local Marine recruiting offices. In a letter he sends to school coaches and physical education teachers, Colonel Hallisey, officer in charge of recruiting in the New York area, writes, "The purpose of our program is to promote noncompetitive physical fitness under the guidance of the local school's physical education department." The program consists of five exercises described in an accompanying brochure and in a film that demonstrates the program. This five-exercise program includes squat thrusts, sit-ups, pull-ups, push-ups, and the shuttle run. The participants are scored and the scores sent to the Marine Corps, which awards certificates of physical achievement. The program has had considerable success in schools coast to coast. Statistics on the number of young men it brought into the Marines are not available, but the Marines insist this program is not a recruiting effort but a public-service venture.

The Marines are also participating in a program established by order of former Secretary of Defense Robert McNamara to bring into the armed forces many of the men who would normally be disqualified from service because they scored poorly on aptitude tests. Project 100,000 has since been extended to include even some men who would normally have been disqualified for physical reasons. The Corps grumbled about the program but bent to the task of making Marines out of these borderline cases. Just how well the Marine decision to comply with Project 100,000 is being accepted at the lower levels of command, at the DI level, is debatable. The DI will find in these men the same problems he finds with other recruits, and it is highly unlikely that the DI will be motivated by any great concern for Project 100,000 when he's trying to roust a sleepy, mentally slow, unmotivated kid out of the rack in the morning.

There is surely some validity to the argument that the Marines can work wonders with problem kids. The comments of Waldo Lyon are appropriate:

> Many a case history could be cited of the town bully who was "squared away" in the Marines. Many a judge, knowing well the abysmal failure of juvenile incarcera-

tion, has ordered the sniveling delinquent to the Marines. For indeed these adolescent youths clearly demand an authoritarian structured environment to contain their dark and unknown impulses. When the structure is lacking throughout childhood and adolescence, we may witness the youth fairly crying out for firmness, while regressing into hippiehood or provoking civilian authority figures.

Thus the Marine Corps satisfies the needs of youth for order, self-control, pride, and accomplishment. And thus the Marine Corps shows the boy he can perform feats of physical courage and stamina he had not dreamed lay in his power. But does the end justify the means? Must we rely on a brutal, anachronistic organization to give the youth that vital feeling of competence and maturity?

Over half a century ago William James, in speaking of the "moral equivalent" of war, stated that fear "is not, as our military enthusiasts believe and try to make us believe, the only stimulus known for awakening the higher ranges of man's spiritual energy." Let us then bring the full force of our national intelligence to the task of reevaluating and rebuilding our military forces into institutions more relevant to today's world. No longer can we be satisfied with the old answers. We must question, question. None of our institutions are so holy that they cannot bear critical examination. As Robert Kennedy said, "the sharpest criticism often goes hand in hand with the greatest idealism and love of country."

In General Chapman's address to the Union League, he talked about Marines, the ones lowest in the ranks, and what those Marines think about the men appointed over them:

> It's pretty difficult for a young rifleman to believe that all senior noncommissioned officers are corrupt, when he has learned to rely on the proven honesty of his Gunnery Sergeant or First Sergeant—especially when these men seem as old as his father, and yet continue to choose to serve in the hardships of combat. Or the Regimental Ser-

geant Major who carries the scars of three wars and
still finds a way to bring mail and cold beer to an isolated outpost. He also finds it hard to believe that the
men who seek commissions are looking for the easy way,
when his own Lieutenant is always the first man into a
a dangerous spot—or his Captain refuses to seek cover so
that he can determine the source of enemy fire.

These things, as the Commandant stated, a young rifleman knows. Surely.

But he knows of *other* noncommissioned Marines, the
ones in whom sadism runs deeper than patriotism, from
whom cruelty springs sooner than valor, with whom service
is hell, not glory, and from whom comes debasing profanity
rather than a call to serve.

These are men who should trouble the Commandant because ultimately these are men who will undermine the
very discipline on which the Marine Corps depends, and
as General Chapman knows and as he stated in the Union
League speech, when discipline breaks down, brutalization
sets in.

CHAPTER THIRTEEN

THE TROUBLED CORPS

*I salute you in the name of the freedom
that you defend and the honor that you
have won for your country.*
President Lyndon B. Johnson

On October 17, 1968, President Lyndon B. Johnson presented the Presidential Unit Citation to the 5th Marines. "I
never think of a Marine but what I think of a man who
wants to do more, not less; a man you have to hold back and
not shove," he said. These remarks were made in a year
when the Marines held Khe Sanh, defended Hue in hard
house-to-house fighting, won ten Congressional Medals of
Honor, and demonstrated that even in the unpopular Vietnam war "uncommon valor was a common virtue," as it had
been at Iwo Jima.

But in 1968, Marines died at home, victims of a Corps
that is flawed and troubled. The honor that valiant Marines earned in combat was tarnished by some of the incidents and events described in this book, but while it is one
thing to uncover the failings of a proud and honored organization such as the Marines, it is quite another to leave
it at that, to make no constructive contribution. To defame

is easy and, today, popular. But the authors have no intention of falling prey to that temptation. In the course of research for this book, we have gotten to know the Marines well, and in some ways we have emerged from the experience with a higher regard for the Marine Corps than we had when we began this work. We found flaws and pointed them out. It may seem, because we have concentrated on those flaws in the writing of this book, that the Marines are beyond help. Not true. While it would be easy and popular in this age of anti-militarism to recommend the abolition of this elite Corps of fighting men, we will not make that recommendation. What we recommend is a series of reforms within the Corps and within the governmental organizations that deal with it. What we believe will result is a finer, prouder, and more honorable Marine Corps.

The cases discussed previously have shown us precise instances in which the Marines can make needed reforms, some sweeping in nature, others more limited but nonetheless important.

"Bagel boy," for example, found himself in difficulty not only because he was a college man and a Jew serving under a cadre with personal prejudices against those characteristics, but also because he was stigmatized as a reservist—a stigma attached to reservists in all the armed forces, but especially in the Marines. Currently, a reservist undergoes basic Marine training with other recruits who are enlistees. Reservists in these circumstances may be singled out for harsh treatment simply because they are reservists. We strongly urge that the Marine Corps establish separate reserve platoons within training battalions at recruit training depots. Because all reservists enter the Corps upon completion of their college educations and train at approximately the same time each year, there will be ample numbers for organizing these separate platoons.

Additionally, these men will adapt more quickly, learn faster, and progress more rapidly than other recruits with less education. By separating them from slower learners, their training can be accelerated and neither group will be antagonized by being in each other's way. Our recommendation: Establish a reservist platoon at all Marine training depots when reservists are entering active duty.

The tragedy of the case of José Concepción is one that will never be fully known because of the manner in which his death was investigated. The lack of an immediate and thorough autopsy makes it impossible to know with certainty how the boy died. There is no excuse whatever for the failure to have a proper autopsy and proper embalming of the body in this case. We believe that there must be mandatory autopsies performed immediately on those who die in the armed services under circumstances such as those in the Concepción case. These must be performed by the medical services of the Defense Department or under their direct supervision. Wherever possible, corpses must be embalmed by the military medical services, not civilian contractors; but if such contractors are used, they must be scrupulously supervised and regulated. Our recommendation: Completely review procedures within the military for handling cases of noncombat, nonmedically attended deaths.

Private José, like so many recruits at Parris Island who get into trouble, had been sent to the Motivation Platoon. This outfit is nothing more than a Marine jail into which a man is put without due process of law and where he is subjected to gross maltreatment, brutality, and physical harassment. Advertised by the Marines as a special unit for handling problem recruits, the Motivation Platoon functions on the theory that a bad boy can be corrected in his errant ways by spanking. Actually, most men who find themselves in Motivation have deep psychological problems of adjustment, not just to the Marines, but to life, and brutality and fear are not the remedies for these men. The Motivation Platoon is in reality a punishment platoon, a place for corporal punishment inflicted without due process of law. These men should be turned over to competent persons who can get at the root of their difficulties and who can either correct them or recommend that the problem recruit be discharged from the Marines. Our recommendation: Abolish the Motivation Platoon.

To deal with the men who now go to Motivation, the Marines should establish adequately staffed psychiatric units with personnel sufficiently trained and with sufficient time to work with problem recruits in the hope that they can be salvaged as Marines. If not, they should be separated from the Marines, for their good and for the good of the Corps. Our recommendation: Substantially increase the staff and scope of the psychiatric unit at Parris Island and at other recruit training depots.

Of course, as many of these problem recruits as possible should be eliminated from the ranks of the Marines as soon as possible, and there is no more likely place to screen out these men than in the recruiting station.

At this level there is need for a better system of screening recruits physically and mentally. These examinations have often been superficial at best. Undertaken by members of the medical services of the armed forces, these examinations are now conducted against the background of pressing needs for quotas to be filled. Our recommendation: Armed forces physical and mental examinations should be conducted by physicians and psychiatrists from the U.S. Department of Health, not the medical services of the armed forces.

The Marine Corps has joined the Defense Department's Project 100,000, a scheme to require all services to accept a certain percentage of inductees who would normally fall below minimum physical and mental qualifications to serve. We believe that many men inducted into the Marine Corps under this program will fail as Marines. Poorly educated, poorly motivated, and poorly suited to be Marines, they will be in trouble immediately and are likely to find themselves in the brig, in Motivation, or over the hill—outlaws. Our recommendation: The Marine Corps should be exempt fom participation in Project 100,000.

We recommend this because we feel that the Marines should be, as intended by law, an elite combat outfit. And because that is the purpose of the Corps, we feel that men entering its service should be given as much encouragement as possible to make the Marines their career. If any of our armed forces is to be a professional service, it should be the Marines. Under present conditions, there is little to encourage men to undertake the Marine Corps as a lifework. We believe incentives should be established to make a Marine career more appealing. For example, a young man entering the Corps at age seventeen, later marrying and beginning a family, will sooner or later weigh his Marine career against the needs of his family, especially of his children's need for a college education. We feel these men should not have to choose between the Corps and their families' needs. Consideration should be given to making government scholarships available to the children of men who serve in the Corps until retirement. Better pay, of course, should be provided as an additional incentive to making the Marines a career. Because we believe the Marine Corps must have higher standards for accepting men into its ranks and should offer handsome incentives to encourage those men to remain with the Corps, we recommend that Congress provide the needed legislation to make these improvements.

A man who joins the Marines sometimes realizes he's made a mistake. Under present enlistments, a man will have to serve two, three, or four years. A young man signing up for four years at the age of seventeen probably will not know with certainty that he wants to be a Marine. Most of the men who get into trouble do so because they rebel against the Corps and its discipline. We think these men should have a way to correct their mistake without going UA or spending most of their enlistment in misery. There should be a period of orientation or adjustment before that final commitment is made to a long period of time in the Marines. Our recommendation: Enlistment in the Marines should be for one year, during which time the enlistee can leisurely decide if he is going to stay in the Corps. If so, his reenlistment could be for a minimum of four years. During his first year, the man will be a basic Marine, receiving no training other than basic combat training. In these months, the recruit will have an opportunity to see if he wants to remain in the Corps, and in what capacity.

Just as the Marines should be regarded as a career, the job of Drill Instructor should be regarded as a career within the Marines. The DI should be the elite among the elite. They must be professional trainers of men, rigorously screened, trained, tested, and retested before they are assigned to boot-training duties. The policy of assigning men to become DI's as just another aspect of their overall Marine experience is a policy that the Corps should change. Being a DI should be the highest achievement available to professional Marines, and proper incentives should be available. Our recommendation: Immediately establish a highly professional staff of Drill Instructors within the Corps.

In the course of research for this book, we have found that the system of military justice in the United States is basically sound. But there are two major flaws that must be corrected immediately. We find it is inconsistent with justice—military and civil—that American servicemen (not just Marines) do not have recourse to bail when arrested and charged with a crime. The denial of the right to bail to men in uniform is clearly a denial of a basic right that must belong to all Americans, whether in uniform or not. We also find it unconscionable that a man merely charged with a crime is confined for long periods of time prior to his trial. That time is irretrievable. If he is convicted, it does not apply against his sentence. If he's acquitted, the time has been spent in prison by a man innocent of any crime. This flagrant injustice should not be permitted any longer in our armed services. Our recommendation: A review of American military justice should be made by the combined Committees on the Judiciary of the House of Representatives and the Senate.

When military justice runs its course and a man is sentenced to prison, he enters hell. Sweeping reforms are needed in the military prison system in the United States. Our recommendation: A Presidential task force on penology should conduct a study of the military penal system and make recommendations for reform.

We make these specific recommendations regarding two of the brigs we studied:

The brig at Parris Island: This old, antiquated building must be closed and a new, modern facility built. Within that building, recruit-detainees must be separated, as now, from regular Marine trainees, but unlike now most aspects of their recruit training should be suspended while they are imprisoned. Professional correctional personnel must replace the present nonprofessional staff.

The Brooklyn brig: The present facility must be closed immediately to remove it from the festering narcotics traffic that has flooded into that facility. The New York area has several government reservations to which the brig can be transferred.

The Brooklyn facility is a scandal. The illegal traffic in narcotics must be ended not only at the brig but also in St. Alban's Naval Hospital. Because the military and Naval authorities have been unable to arrest this insidious traffic, we urgently recommend that the Federal Bureau of Narcotics clean up the situation. A healthy way to begin would be with a raid on those facilities.

We found that unnecessary red tape frequently separates a man in the brig from religious counseling. There should be no delay in any brig between a man's request to see a chaplain or to have a Bible and the granting of his request.

Like the military penal system, the chaplains' corps in our armed forces has existed for many years with little attention paid to its purpose and its work. We recommend an examination of the role of the chaplain in our armed forces by a panel of civilian religious leaders of all faiths.

We have already recommended in a previous chapter a Presidential commission of enlisted personnel from all armed forces to study the racial problems confronting the armed forces. There should be no delay in establishing this commission.

Because there is usually a gap in communication between a man in the lower ranks of our armed forces and his commanders, the lowly enlisted man feels alone and helpless confronting the vast American military. Appeals for help when made through existing channels go unheard or become hopelessly bogged down in red tape. We suggest that a man who needs help needs help right now, not later. Therefore, we have given considerable thought to how this might be achieved. For a man in uniform to express a grievance against his commanders is difficult, often impossible. It should not be. If anyone ever needed and deserved an ombudsman, it is the ordinary GI. Therefore, we recommend establishment of a military ombudsman division with the U.S. Department of Justice. A staff of competent federal attorneys should be available to our men in uniform, and these attorneys should be available on each military installation. We recommend that a civilian ombudsman from the Department of Justice be installed at every military and Naval facility and that access to the ombudsman be unimpaired. These men would function in the same way as federal attorneys in the existing civil-rights division of the Justice Department and would provide an effective and healthy additional civilian check on the military.

Our Constitution wisely establishes a system of checks and balances among the three branches of our government. The Congress has the power to regulate the armed forces, and as we have shown, that power lies heavily upon the House Committee on Armed Services. As noted earlier, this committee, because of its long association with the Defense Department, has become virtually an arm of the Pentagon. There is a "credibility gap" that must be eliminated if the people of the United States are to have confidence in the ability of the Congress to keep a check on the military establishment. The House Armed Services Committee has often failed in its primary responsibility of being a watchdog over the Pentagon. There is no greater symbol of this situation than Major General John R. Blandford, chief counsel of the committee.

It seems to us that Blandford's duties as chief counsel are in conflict with his commission as a major general in the United States Marine Corps Reserves. It is hard to imagine a situation that raises more serious questions of conflict of interest than this one, and we recommend that General Blandford resign his post with the committee immediately.

Similarly, some members of Congress appear to have the same conflict of interest because they also hold commissions in the reserves. That Congress must vote on military matters is essential to the system of checks and balances, but when members of Congress also serve in the reserves of the very armed forces they are required under law to regulate, it seems to be a gross conflict of interest.

We do not recommend—we *demand*—that every member of Congress now serving in any capacity in the armed forces reserves end that service.

We demand the enactment of legislation to prohibit members of Congress from serving in the armed forces reserves while they also hold Congressional office.

We demand enactment of legislation to prohibit service in the reserves of the armed forces by any members of the staffs of Congressmen and Senators who sit on the House and Senate Armed Services Committees.

Finally, because he has become a symbol of an unhealthy accommodation between the Department of Defense and the House Committee on Armed Services, we urge, for the good of the committee and the military, that Representative L. Mendel Rivers relinquish his chairmanship of that committee.

All of these recommendations, we believe, will improve the conditions under which men and women serve in the armed forces of the United States. Furthermore, they will revitalize America's faith in her armed forces.

We know that brutality and sadism will not disappear from the ranks of our military until brutality and sadism disappear from the hearts of mankind, but we regret that the United States Marine Corps has given only lip service to words condemning sadism and brutality. Men found guilty of maltreatment have been given light sentences, many of which were further reduced. Commanders look the other way, condoning maltreatment and brutality. When pressed to explain why brutality is permitted, the Marine Corps replies that these are isolated incidents that are condemned and punished by the Corps. Public-relations efforts are then mounted to correct not the condition that breeds brutality but the tarnished image that results.

The United States Marine Corps suffers from a crisis of confidence that is surely as deep as that which followed that awful night in 1956 when DI Matthew McKeon marched six Marines to their death. Official Marine proclamations that brutality will not be condoned sound hollow against the ringing truth of the brutality that *does* exist and *is* condoned.

It is time for the Marine Corps to be honest, to abandon its defensive posture when the question of brutality is raised, and to admit that its policy at present does condone maltreatment and brutalization.

The time has come for the Commandant to back up his words and his official policies against brutality with strict, swift, and unrelenting enforcement of those policies.

Unless the United States Marine Corps drops its pretense that brutality does not exist and is not condoned, the Corps is merely biding its time until another Drill Instructor marches a platoon of vulnerable recruits—and the Corps—to disaster.

CHAPTER FOURTEEN

McKEON REVISITED

*It's coming closer to the day when I'm
going to meet those kids.*

Matthew C. McKeon

The United States Marine Corps is haunted.

Ghosts of six young recruits roam through the ranks of the Corps, and it is as if time itself were measured by the hour of their deaths—a dark, damp moment in the murky waters of Ribbon Creek on Parris Island in the chilly April springtime of 1956.

The ghosts also haunt Matthew C. McKeon, a man whose name will forever be linked to the ominous words "death march."

Every instance of brutality, sadism, hazing, or other maltreatment of recruits at Parris Island will stir awful memory of that night when Sergeant Matt McKeon marched seventy-five sleepy young Marine recruits into Ribbon Creek and caused the deaths of six of them by drowning. All the Marine Corps regulations against physical and mental maltreatment sprang from that incident. Every Drill Instructor walks in the shadow of the man found guilty of negligence in those deaths. Every recruit looks at the straight-backed

201

DI standing ramrod-stiff in front of his platoon and wonders, "Is he one of them? One of the bad ones?"

Matthew McKeon knows all of this, thinks about it, and on rare occasions, talks about it.

He talked with the authors of this book about it:

> AUTHORS: Matt, how would you compare recruit training today with training before Ribbon Creek?
>
> MCKEON: It's changed. After that incident, it has changed.
>
> AUTHORS: How?
>
> MCKEON: I was talking to recruits coming out of Parris Island after the incident, but before I got out of the Corps myself. And looking at them. I'm afraid that today. . . . Just for instance, if a kid was walking down a company street, walking around the installation, and he had his sleeves rolled up or his hat on the back of his head? Years ago, if a corporal met this kid, right then and there he'd correct the kid. He'd square the kid away. But today when a corporal sees a *lieutenant* allow this kid to walk by with his sleeves rolled up and not correct him, then why should the corporal step up and do it? It looks to me from what I could see, everybody is running a popularity contest.
>
> AUTHORS: You mean things are not as good in the Corps today, Matt?
>
> MCKEON: Yeah. I'll be truthful and say that there are a hell of a lot of good Marines today. They must be, they're showing it in Vietnam, aren't they? But the big thing today is the racism. I think the Commandant dropped the ball in the eyes of a lot of Marines when he allowed a certain segment to wear the Afro-American haircut.

And that isn't right. It was one of the most horrible mistakes.

AUTHORS: What do you think it's going to do to the Corps?

MCKEON: What it's going to do to the Corps is what it would do to any organization. An organization only functions as well as the morale in it. If the morale is down, then the outfit is down. What is the difference to this man in an Afro-American haircut or a regulation haircut? What about the rights of the white kid who wants to let his hair grow long? Why can't he let it grow long? There's got to be some uniform code there. I think it's going to demoralize the Marine Corps. The Marine Corps had one thing going for it. Know what it was? Esprit de corps. Once you destroy esprit de corps, then you destroy the Corps itself.

AUTHORS: You never lost your feeling for the Marine Corps despite what happened to you, did you?

MCKEON: No, I never will.

AUTHORS: Were you ever bitter about what happened?

MCKEON: No, not really. I was bitter in respect to the shame I brought upon the Marine Corps and upon my family. That's the only thing I was bitter about. As regarding myself, no. My own personal feelings, never. I don't believe there's any ex-Marines. I believe once a Marine, always a Marine. Seriously. I talk to a lot of ex-Marines and they're all Marines.

AUTHORS: How has it been? It's been fourteen years. That's a long time. Were you ever able to forget the incident?

MCKEON: No, never. Never.

AUTHORS: When you think about it, what do you think about?

MCKEON: It's coming closer to the day when I'm going to meet those kids.

AUTHORS: What do you mean by that?

MCKEON: Well, I'm getting older, and someday I'm going to pass on. I believe I'll meet them. I only hope that they forgive me. I pray for them. I never forget them.

AUTHORS: Did you ever blame yourself for that?

MCKEON: Blame myself for it, sir? No, not really. Never.

As he spoke, a curious transformation came over this forty-five-year-old man who now lives quietly, anonymously with his family, holding down a government job in Massachusetts, residing in a neighborhood that houses some other former Marines. Recalling the days at Parris Island, McKeon may have been hearing again the clipped cadence of his own voice barking out the marching beat for a platoon of skinheads. A crispness came into the voice that wasn't there before, as if he were calling that voice to attention. He began saying "sir."

AUTHORS: What were your thoughts as a DI, Matt?

MCKEON: Sir, I thought if I could put out one good Marine, then I'd figure I'd done something.

AUTHORS: A lot of people think you put out a lot of good Marines, Matt.

MCKEON: They're all good Marines, sir. But I don't know what's happening in the Marine Corps. I suppose what's happening in the Marine Corps is what's happening all over the country.

AUTHORS: Matt, when you meet other old-timers, what do you talk about with them?

MCKEON: [laughing] There's a couple of 'em live across the street. We get laughing, you know, about funny incidents? We never really talk about the bad things or the bad times or the hard times. There's always something. The fellow across the street went in on Guadalcanal. We just talk. We just talk Marine talk. We see the kids here on the street, and we tell them they're not hackin' it. Or once in a while we tell them to fall back and regroup. If they get out of hand, the guys across the street will say, "Lads, you better fall back and regroup." We talk Marines. The guy across the street is a great friend of General Walt. He was sorry that Walt didn't get Commandant.

AUTHORS: What do you think of Chapman as a Commandant?

MCKEON: I don't know the gentleman. I know Walt very well. You'd better not mention my name to Walt [laughter]. I was under his command a couple of times. Of the two evils, I'd just as soon have seen Walt make Commandant.

AUTHORS: You don't have any love for either of them?

MCKEON: Well, I didn't know Chapman. But I knew Walt. Of the two evils I'd prefer Walt. I think Chapman lost a lot in giving in.

AUTHORS: On what issue, Matt?

MCKEON: The racial issue. He lost a tremendous amount.

AUTHORS: Do you have any sons, Matt?

MCKEON: I have one. Fourteen years old.

AUTHORS: When it comes time for service, are you going to recommend the Marines to him?

MCKEON: I definitely will, but he doesn't seem too

military-minded. It seems like the farthest thing from his mind. He's quite an athlete.

AUTHORS: If you were going to write a book about the Marines, what would you want to say in that book?

MCKEON: Discipline. If they could inspire discipline in any unit. In the Marine Corps they get discipline by fear. I say 75 or 80 per cent of the discipline was fear. Without discipline you don't have any obedience. Without obedience you have no respect. If you don't have any respect, you might as well secure. That's what made the Marine Corps. You can say all you want about anything else, but discipline made the Marine Corps.

AUTHORS: After Ribbon Creek, they came up with all kinds of changes, and they did come up with some new guidelines for DI's. Did you feel they went too easy?

MCKEON: Certainly. I say they did, sir.

AUTHORS: In what way?

MCKEON: They took away from the DI the one big weapon he had. Fear. He could not harass them anymore. No more hazing. No more physical punishment like duck waddling or crawling or creeping on your gut. No bucket over the head for the smokers. When they took away the tools that a Marine DI has had down the years to make good Marines, it had to hurt something. Basically, sir, what the Marine Corps did to the DI's is what the Supreme Court is doing to the police of this country.

AUTHORS: Taking their power away?

MCKEON: That's right, sir. You know, when you were a kid you respected a policeman. You had to. Maybe not for any other reason but that you feared him. But today the Supreme Court has taken away that fear and in the same way the Commandant is taking away the tools of fear that a DI has.

AUTHORS: Do people remember you, Matt? And what do they say to you?

MCKEON: Every now and then someone will come up and say they know me. I shake their hands. They say we were on your side, or you got a raw deal. And I try to tell them I didn't get a raw deal. I tell them I was wrong in some respect. If they blaspheme the Corps, I tell them, no. They're all good. All Marines are good.

A few years ago, Matt McKeon was invited to attend a convention of the Marine Corps League, meeting in Albany, New York. He went, but when they wanted him to speak, he declined. So several hundred Marines and former Marines stood and applauded him. Then the band struck up their song.

APPENDIX 1

Parris Island

"This is Parris Island," says a Marine brochure. "The primary mission of the Marine Corps Recruit Depot, Parris Island, is to train recruits. It is ordinarily the first military station seen by recruits from east of the Mississippi River following their enlistment. The primary purpose of the training is to indoctrinate the recruit with the essential knowledge derived from almost two centuries of experience in training fighting men, and to inculcate in the individual that intangible esprit de corps that is the hallmark of United States Marines."

The recruit arriving at Parris Island does, indeed, step into history, and although the first Marine Corps activity on Parris Island did not occur until 1891, the island itself is steeped in American history. First discovered by the Spaniard Lucas Vazquez de Ayllon in 1526, it became in 1562 a French outpost in the New World. The first title to Parris Island was granted to Major Robert Daniell in 1700, and in 1715 the land passed into the possession of Alexander Parris. Marines didn't land on the island until June 26, 1891, when a small detachment was posted for duty with a Naval station. In 1915 the Marines took over the island and established the Recruit Training Depot. During World War I, 41,000 Marines trained at the base. Not until 1929 were a bridge and causeway built as an access to the island, all travel prior to that time having been by boat. In August, 1940, battalion-size training was begun at PI, as the Marines call the island, and with the coming of World War II a flood of men deluged the base, forcing enlargement of its facilities to handle thirteen recruit battalions. Between 1941 and 1945, 202,000 recruits trained at PI. Another 20,000 were in training at the time of the Japanese surrender. Postwar demobilization brought the doldrums to PI, but the beginning of the Korean conflict soon fleshed out the ranks once more, swelling the Parris Island population from 2,350 to a peak of 24,424 in March of 1952. The Korean War saw more than 138,000 Marines trained at PI. As a thoroughgoing training base, the Parris Island Recruit Depot was a vital arm of the Corps, functioning with little fanfare or public attention, except for those families whose sons or husbands were stationed at the facility, until the McKeon case put Parris Island in the headlines.

Depending on one's reasons for going to the island, PI can be a beautiful historical excursion or a lonely, frightening ride into the unknown. The island is reached only after a long ride by car or bus down a palmetto-lined highway dubbed "the scenic route" by the South Carolina tourist bureau but pointedly described by a whimsical Marine with a sign posted at an intersection: TO KHE SANH.

The nearest town to Parris Island is Beaufort, South Carolina, a sleepy community that might serve as a location for one of Tennessee Williams' plays about remnants of the Old South. Beaufort (pronounced "Bewfort") is as Southern as its grand antebellum houses and century-old gardens, halfway between Charleston and Savannah.

The Marine Training Depot at Parris Island operates at a cost to the taxpayers of $24,612,602 (fiscal year 1970). Of this amount, $16,373,028 was earmarked for military

personnel, $4,997,000 for civilian personnel, and $3,242,-
574 for other operational needs. The total figure is lower
than that for fiscal year 1969, and about the same as that for
fiscal year 1968.

What the taxpayers get for this money, say the Marines,
is the finest military training establishment in the world
turning out the finest military product in history—a 1970
Marine.

The facilities at Parris Island house the Recruit Training Regiment, which is composed of three battalions of
recruits and a Weapons Training Battalion. Also located
at the base is the only battalion designated for training of
women Marines. PI also houses a Drill Instructors School,
Recruiters School, Field Music School, Administration
School, and Sergeants Major School. Without question, Parris Island is the Marine Corps's most important training
facility.

But for the raw recruit rattling down the way marked
by both the "scenic route" and "Khe Sanh" signs, Parris Island is a conglomeration of all the tales he has heard
from other Marines, all the John Wayne war movies he
has seen on the Late Show on TV, all the Corps's recruiting posters and pamphlets, all his own dreams of being a
man, of proving himself, of finding fulfillment in snappy
Marine dress blues, and all the fears any human feels
when he is venturing into the unknown.

The bus carrying the recruit proceeds through the main
gate and then crosses a bridge heading for the recruit receiving building.

"If there's quite a few of them on the bus," says Captain
M. R. Arnold, public information officer at Parris Island,
"then they will fall out of the bus, line up on the yellow
footprints that are painted on the deck outside. One at a
time they will file into a building and stand alongside
tables, placing their right hands on a number that is

painted on the table. This number gives them a position within the room to stay in."

Emptying everything out of their pockets, the recruits wait at their numbers while a Drill Instructor examines the contents they have laid out on the table, examining the objects for those items a Marine recruit may keep. He looks for two things: any papers or documents that the recruit will need or that may need attention, such as a still-unpaid civilian traffic ticket, and any contraband. The list of contraband items includes firearms, blackjacks or razors, alcoholic beverages, playing cards, obscene literature, chewing gum, jewelry other than watches, and any items containing glass.

"If they have framed pictures or pictures that won't go in their wallet," explains Captain Arnold, "those are taken away and sent home."

While the recruit is sorting out his personal belongings, he receives his first formal lesson as a recruit, a short lecture delivered by a DI on the Uniform Code of Military Justice, the first of many lectures he will receive on the law by which the United States armed forces are governed and by which a recruit will be judged if he errs.

At this time, also, the recruit receives his first article of Marine clothing, a utility jacket, a rugged waist-length coat known in other military branches as a field jacket. The recruit also gets a towel, an item he will find useful in the next few moments of his life at PI.

What follows is easily the most harrowing experience of the young recruit's initiation into the Corps—the fastest haircut in the world. In forty-five seconds or less, the recruit is shorn of the long hair he has customarily worn as a civilian. With swift, deft, and deep strokes, a barber shears away the locks, cutting down to the skin and leaving the recruit as bald as electric clippers can make a man.

After the haircut the recruit goes into the shower to

scrub the scalp that has been buried beneath the mass of hair that now lies in a heap on the floor of the barber shop. If he has a beard or mustache, it too disappears at this time.

Clean-shaven and bald, the recruit heads to another location to receive more Marine clothing—skivvies, socks, and boots. He heads back to his place at the numbered tables in the receiving barracks, strips, discarding his civilian clothing, and puts on his new issue. The discarded clothing may be sent home in bundles that the recruits pack themselves at this time, or it may be given to Goodwill Industries. Stripped except for skivvies, socks, and boots, the recruit waits at his number while the DI's who have been processing the recruits pass along the ranks painting a number on each recruit's chest and hand, the number marking each man's place in the line for the remainder of the in-processing.

Now nearing the end of processing, the recruit goes through various administrative routines—being photographed for an identification card, making arrangements for allotments to be deducted from his pay, and having various needed innoculations. He receives the final issue of clothing, not including any dress uniforms. He gets only the basic work uniform, Marine-green dungarees and shirts, cap, underwear, and so on. No dress uniforms are issued because each Marine will undergo marked changes in his physique, either gaining or losing weight in the next eight weeks of training.

Up to this point, the recruits have been under the control of Drill Instructors, who have been concerned only with the efficient processing of the men. In one of the great understatements encountered in our research into Marine life, Captain Arnold remarked, "There will be a rather marked difference between the way the Drill Instructor in the receiving barracks handles the recruit and the way the Drill Instructor that picks them up in a platoon will handle them."

Leaving the receiving barracks by the rear door, the recruit falls into a formation to await the arrival of the man who will, over the next two months, hold his fate in his hands—his platoon Drill Instructor.

"He starts out with a very loud voice," says Captain Arnold, "and a very insistent-persistent voice. From there on out, he is in absolute control. He uses his main control tool—his vocal cords."

The first command the new recruit hears from his DI is the call to attention.

From this point on, the voices of the Drill Instructor and his two Assistant Drill Instructors will measure the moments of a recruit's existence. There are only two aspects of his life that a recruit will count as sacred and safe from a DI's interference—his meals and his sleep. No matter what else is happening, the Marine recruit will eat and sleep on time. Every other moment belongs to the DI.

"Your ass," says the DI, "belongs to me."

But not entirely.

The recruit has a rigorous schedule that he must follow. Every hour of that schedule is listed in a Recruit Training Schedule issued by the Recruit Training Regiment Headquarters. This fifteen-page mimeographed document contains all the dates, times, and other pertinent information that a DI will need to guide a platoon of recruits through basic Marine training. The schedule begins with physical exams at 0730 on the first day of training and accounts for all time in the eight weeks until the recruit leaves PI at 1000 on the day of his graduation from boot camp. Nothing is left to chance.

The man in charge of overseeing the coordination of training for the three recruit training battalions functioning at any one time at PI is the commanding officer, Recruit Training Regiment, Colonel Robert J. Perrich, a square-jawed, crew-cut, mustachioed Marine veteran. Colonel Perrich assumed his duties as recruit commanding officer on July 18, 1969. He served with the 3d Marine Division in Vietnam and holds the Vietnamese Cross of Gallantry. Among his other medals are the Presidential Unit Citation, World War II Victory Medal, China Service Medal, Korean Presidential Unit Citation, Korean Service Medal with two battle stars, and the National Defense Service Medal. A Californian, Colonel Perrich is forty-six years of age and a graduate of the U.S. Naval Academy. From his office in a cantaloupe-colored two-story building in the heart of the base, Colonel Perrich commands the men who inhabit what the Marines describe as "one of the most efficient and picturesque military reservations in the world."

Colonel Perrich's immediate superior officer is the commanding general, Marine Corps Recruit Depot, Major General Oscar F. Peatross. Balding, bespectacled, fifty-four-year-old O. F. Peatross is also a veteran of Marine Corps combat. Having served with the Second Marine Raider Battalion operating from submarines, he earned the Navy Cross for his action during the Makin Island raid. He served at Guadalcanal, Bougainville, and Iwo Jima, earning the Bronze Star Medal with Combat "V." In postwar years he served as an instructor at various military schools and rose to the rank of lieutenant colonel in 1951. His next assignment took him to Korea as a battalion commander, Second Battalion, 5th Marines. Returning to training assignments in the States after Korea, Peatross reached the rank of full colonel and then went on duty in Vietnam, where he participated in actions at Chu Lai and commanded the 7th Regiment, earning an assortment of Vietnamese medals. He was promoted to brigadier general in 1966 and to major general in 1968. One of his two sons enlisted in the Marines and completed his tour in the Corps in June, 1968. His second son has yet to decide whether he'll be a Marine.

General Peatross is a realist when it comes to training men for what they will encounter in combat, which, he points out, is the sole purpose of the Marines. "When we make a beachhead," he says with great forcefulness, "there's no leave, there's no liberty, there's no Coke machine, there's no candy machine, no radio, no TV, no access to snack bars. Our training is based precisely on the philosophy of what a man will have to do when he makes an amphibious operation, so here at Parris Island there won't be any candy machines and the cakes and Cokes and TV. Not to punish the man, but to test his character to see whether or not he can perform as he's supposed to do in combat."

General Peatross admits, a little sadly, that the Corps has lowered its standards in accepting men into its ranks. Noting that prior to World War II the Corps had high and rigid physical requirements for recruits as well as requiring all of them to be at least high school graduates, Peatross states that under those conditions virtually every recruit would make it readily through Parris Island training. With standards lowered because of the need for men for Vietnam, Peatross says there is no question that more men fail the Marine training system today than previously. Dropout rates now run about 5 per cent, he says. Others said the figure was 8 per cent or higher.

As all Marines do, no matter what their special gripes may be about the Corps, General Peatross speaks with pride in the Corps, its mission, and the way it carries out that mission. "I think," he says, "that there are three points I would like to stress about the Marines. First, our system of training enlisted personnel. Second, the system of training officers. Third, the techniques and developments the Marine Corps actually makes. Some people don't realize how technical the Marine Corps is. I don't think the public knows that some two thousand of our total Marine Corps are involved in the computer system alone. You take the joint unified military pay which the Department of Defense started to work on sometime ago, and you find that the Marine Corps led the way. The Marines developed and perfected the amphibious technique which the Germans gave up on in World War II. This is a technique that unquestionably we developed. The Marines were the first to have helicopters, and their use has been one of the biggest breakthroughs in the history of the military since I've been in it."

It is this pride in the Corps that General Peatross hopes to instill in the raw recruits who come into Parris Island with their fashionably long hair, bell-bottom jeans, and pampered ways.

"At the end of eight, nine, or ten weeks," says General Peatross, "we must end up with a product that's qualified to take over one of the more than four hundred military occupation specialties that we have in the Marines. He should be physically fit to perform duty on the battlefield. When a man leaves here, he should be physically fit, and he should be basically trained in the military customs and courtesies of the service. And by that I mean doing what he's told to do and when he's told to do it. I'm a firm believer in the fact that you've got to test his character. You can't count on a man who's going over the hill. You can't count on a man who can't do without Cokes or candy. I think we get a man out of here that's physically fit and whose mental standards and character have been tested. That essentially is the man we want in the Marine Corps."

> The one thing you must do is drive the wristbone here and this knuckle into his throat. If it is anywhere else, you're not going to choke him. That bayonet's going to go on right through his kidney. Lift it up, slit his throat, and solidly lay him down on the deck without any problem whatsoever. Any questions before we start practicing?

He is short, about 5 feet 3 inches. Bald. A little chubby. Yet he can put a 6-foot 2-inch Marine on the deck with ease, and if the Marine were an enemy and not a recruit, the Drill Instructor could slit his throat with as much ease. He is, however, giving instructions in hand-to-hand combat, and the young recruits who watch and participate are enthralled by the mechanics of how to kill a man.

The Recruit Training Regiment at Parris Island is broken down into three training battalions, which, in turn, consist of basic training units known as Recruit Training Series, each commanded by a lieutenant. Under him are four recruit platoons, each commanded by a lieutenant and each with three Drill Instructors—a Chief DI and two Assistant DI's. Three or four Recruit Training Series make up a company of about one thousand men, all of whom are going through the same training together.

Lieutenant Colonel Richard B. Tuohy is commanding officer of the Second Recruit Training Battalion. One of the most colorful officers in the Corps, Colonel Tuohy is forty-three years of age and regards himself as a "loyal and faithful New Yorker except when the weather gets bad." He was born in New Rochelle but lived mostly in Manhattan. Colonel Tuohy is an ardent activist when it comes to being fit. He rides a bicycle everywhere he goes on the base and is one of the few men who can maintain his dignity on a bike or, as happened once during the course of research at PI on this book, be dignified when he falls *off* the bike before the eyes of a parading platoon. The colonel believes the Corps has an obligation to look after a man's soul as well as his body, although he hastens to point out that the Corps does not force a man to attend religious services. "I encourage them to go because I've never seen anybody hurt inside a church or synagogue. For those who do not wish to go, they do not have to go. In the hour while the others are away at services, those who chose not to go are gainfully employed by doing such things as washing clothes, which seems a useful thing to do. They are not penalized."

Colonel Tuohy has seen to it that "grace" cards are placed on the tables in the mess halls in his battalion, but he says these are there for the convenience of any recruits who want them. Nobody is forced to pray.

"We don't force, we encourage. It would seem rather appropriate. Our country was begun on a religious basis. It is intertwined in the fabric of our nation, and I suspect here that we certainly would give it an opportunity to flourish. I personally encourage it."

Chaplains are available to the recruits at Parris Island, but the time available to recruits to call on them is rather limited.

Recruit training goes through five phases: *Recruit receiving; Phase I*—basic military subjects; *Phase II*—weapons training; *Mess and Maintenance*—KP and other service chores; *Phase III*—classroom work and preparation for graduation. In eight weeks, there are 309 hours of formal instruction, 134 hours for administrative work, 444 hours with Drill Instructors. With the DI, the recruit will have fifty-four hours of physical conditioning, including running the obstacle course, eight hours of water survival, and riflery.

MY RIFLE

This is my rifle. There are many like it, but this one is mine. My rifle is my best friend. It is my life. I must master it as I master my life.

My rifle, without me, is useless. Without my rifle, I am useless. I must fire my rifle true. I must shoot straighter than my enemy who is trying to kill me. I must shoot him before he shoots me. *I will. . . .*

My rifle and myself know that what counts in this war is not the rounds we fire, the noise of our burst, nor the smoke we make. We know that it is the hits that count. We will hit. . . .

My rifle is human, even as I, because it is my life. Thus, I will learn it as a brother. I will learn its weakness, its strength, its parts, its accessories, its sights, and its barrel. I will keep my rifle clean and ready, even as I am clean and ready. We will become part of each other. We will. . . .

Before God I swear this creed. My rifle and myself are defenders of my country. We are the masters of our enemy. We are the saviors of my life.

So be it, until victory is America's and there is no enemy, but Peace!

Except for physical training (PT), nothing takes more of a recruit's time than rifle training. And although there will be many Americans, especially in this day and age, who will shudder at the chauvinism of the above creed, there is no Marine who has ever been in battle who will not agree with the basic sentiment of the creed—that without his rifle a Marine will be dead.

Recruits spend two weeks in weapons training with the Weapons Battalion at Parris Island, most of it with the rifle, although they also receive instruction in other weapons. At the end of this period of instruction, the recruit "fires for record," and the score that he gets remains forever on his service record. As long as he is a Marine, he will fire a rifle for record once a year.

If weapons training instills in the Marine recruit a reliance on a weapon for survival, the Marine Corps's physical training program instills in the recruit a reliance on his own body, on his confidence in himself.

CONFIDENCE COURSE

Made up of several different obstacles, each more difficult to accomplish than the other, it gives the recruit an opportunity to test his confidence and strength.

With its usual understatement, the Marines include the above description of the Confidence Course in the "graduating class" books offered for sale to each recruit on completion of his boot training. It's on the order of a high school yearbook, including photos of the class members, those who have made it.

One of the more formidable obstacles on the Confidence Course is a wire or rope strung across water to simulate a rope or cable crossing that a Marine might encounter in combat. The water below is four feet deep, just enough to make a good cushion for those who fall. Should a Marine fall into the cold water, he is, according to the Marines, sent back to his barracks for a change of clothing. In practice, he goes back up and tries again until he makes it, wet clothes and all. In South Carolina's chilly winters, it can be a bone-chilling ordeal.

"The tough one," says a Marine officer, "is a forty-foot tower that carries a man up to a rope that he must climb down. Well, of course, for a man who has any fear of heights, this is rather a formidable obstacle."

The Confidence Course is run a number of times, confidence, presumably, building each time. If confidence isn't built, a recruit may be threatened with jail, a threat that usually impels the recruit to try harder.

> This is what an average recruit's day looks like: Reveille is a 0455 in the morning. As soon as he gets up, he has approximately five minutes of PT, stretch wake-up exercises that he does right in front of his bunk. He has until 0700 to eat his breakfast, get back, and clean up his squad bay. He begins training at 0700 and will go until 1130 or 1200, depending on his schedule. Normally, the first hour from 0700 to 0800 is PT out on the PT field.

At the very beginning of recruit training, each man undergoes a strength test. This shows his physical ability at the start of training and provides a comparison for the strength test the recruit will take at the end of his boot training. PT is aimed at preparing the recruit for that final test.

But his physical stamina is tested every moment of every day, not simply on the PT field.

Hours are spent on close-order drill.

"Hwan, hup, threep, fo, yo lef'," rings out everywhere at PI. It is the heavy chanting cadence of the DI, heard from dawn to dusk.

"Each DI takes an interest in how his platoon performs on the drill field," explains Captain Arnold, Parris Island's public information officer, "and he takes great pride in their performance."

Along with drill, the DI works hard on the Manual of Arms, the basic assumption being that to use a rifle properly you have to know how to hold it.

Care and keeping of pack and equipment is also a major concern of the DI, and hours are spent by recruits packing and unpacking the gear.

During the training cycle, the DI will be rated by an inspection team that makes unexpected visits at all hours of the day or night.

All of these things occur in what the Marines call the "fifty-minute hour." Out of every hour in the training day, fifty minutes are spent in some phase of training. The other ten minutes are for rest, although rest is largely a matter for the DI to define.

Because Marines are Marines, they are expected to know how to survive in water. Every Marine is taught how to swim and how to keep alive in the water. Seven out of eight hours in water instruction are actually spent in the water in one of the largest indoor pools in the country—700,000 gallons.

The pace is rigorous and the demands are great, and

there is no room or patience for the recruit who can't keep up. Consequently, the Marine Training Depot has established special training groups for problem recruits.

A Conditioning Platoon is divided into two sections, one for handling overweight problems and one for strength problems. One builds up the man who scores poorly on his initial strength test. The other pares down a man who is too fat to be a Marine. This may take up to three months, but even later the overweight recruit maintains a weight watcher's diet when he is back in regular training with a platoon.

A Medical Rehabilitation Platoon reconditions and repairs recruits who have been injured or ill during their training. The chief medical problem at PI is what the Marines call "stress fractures" of the heels, minor bone damage because of the ceaseless marching, drills, and PT.

From time to time, the Corps uses an Orientation Platoon to deal with non-English speaking recruits, mostly Puerto Ricans. Spanish-speaking DIs work with these men, most of whom have been drafted into the Corps, so that they can achieve a competency in English that will allow them to join regular training platoons.

There is, additionally, a Special Training Branch, which gives crash courses for extraordinary problem cases. There is a close connection between this branch and the base neuropsychiatric section. Three psychiatrists and three psychologists work with these special cases.

Chief of the neuropsychiatric section is Navy Lieutenant Commander Frank Forstoeffel. His unit sees an average of fifty recruits a day, most of them men who have an adjustment problem to the Corps and its discipline. Forstoeffel believes that Marine training must be tough and that it is not destructive. He regrets that there is not a better screening process at the recruiting level.

In addition to these special platoons for problem recruits, there is the Motivation Platoon.

To the Motivation Platoon go two types of recruits, the aggressive and the dependent. The latter are more abundant. They are youths who have led sheltered, pampered lives and who are overwhelmed by the austerity and severity of discipline required of them as recruits. They often burst into tears. The aggressive recruits are those who enter the Corps with a chip on their shoulders and who choose to ignore military authority. "Motivation" is the Corps's answer to these problem children.

"They are told about the Marine Corps, the traditions; shown movies, combat movies; taken on motivation hikes, in which they get motivation talks about different areas of interest around here," explained a Marine officer.

Again, the Marines understate.

The hikes to which the officer refers are not hikes but runs, several miles a day, from the Motivation Platoon barracks to two Parris Island monuments—a commemoration of the flag-raising at Iwo Jima and "Iron Mike," an idealized statue of a Marine hero. The recruits run to these symbols of Marine glory and run back, do PT, run out to the monuments, return, and so on throughout the day.

"Motivation" is not a jail. It is highly intensified physical training for a period of up to thirty days.

"There's no bars on the windows or doors," says a Marine captain, "but they are treated more or less in the prison status, kept under close supervision."

Between 1961 and 1968, Navy Lieutenant Commander Waldo B. Lyon was depot psychologist at Parris Island. He had daily opportunities to observe the various special training units functioning at the base. In a paper delivered to the American Orthopsychiatric Association in 1969, he discussed Marine Corps treatment of the maladjusted Marine:

A look into the past revealed the unit for maladjusted Marine recruits at Parris Island in 1962 to be an ex-

tremely militaristic and extremely hostile setting with more
severe discipline than in the unit for recalcitrant unmotivated recruits or in the brig. Recruits with moderate character disorders or immaturity reactions were placed in a
padded cell without due process on orders of the psychiatrist in charge. Physical harassment was condoned on the
basis that this sort of "treatment" was appropriate for
these recruits. This prostituted psychiatric organization
was highly regarded by the Marines. Even a series of de-
fenestrations from the second story failed to dim the
popularity of the unit. By 1966, new leadership had transformed this unit into a psychiatric holding ward while
relegating to Marines the task of "motivating" recalcitrant
recruits.

Upon reading Lyon's paper, a psychiatrist in St. Louis
wrote to him, "While many features of Marine Corps life
do create some positive values, these are too readily over-
stated. The delinquent entering the Marines often finds
ways of perpetuating his delinquency except that now it is
done skillfully and under orders."

One of the lectures a recruit receives in "Motivation"
comes when he is taken to a graduation exercise. "They'll
take them over to watch a graduation," explained Captain
Arnold, "and there they are told that with effort on their
part they can, in so many weeks, cross the parade ground
wearing a uniform and leave Parris Island a Marine."

> Final review is one long to be remembered. The re-
> cruit is now a full-fledged Marine and proud of the fact
> that he has completed the toughest recruit training course
> in the world. While doing so, he has made many lifelong
> friends who share his accomplishments.

The quotation above is *not* Marine overstatement. It is
true.

"Would you ever do it again?" we asked a Marine graduating in February, 1970.

"Well, I believe I would," the Marine private said
smartly.

"How was the training?"

"The training is rough but not too bad. Any normal person can get through it. No problems."

"You're glad you did it?"

"Yes, sir. Very much so."

There was no doubt that the young Marine—now, for the first time he could be called a Marine—was proud to be wearing the uniform that several weeks earlier he had decided, for whatever reasons of his own, he wanted—or needed—to wear, and there was also no doubt that he would be one of the millions of men who have felt a thrill of personal pride in their achievement when they heard the words:

> "If the Army and the Navy
> Ever look on Heaven's scenes,
> They will find the streets are guarded by
> THE UNITED STATES MARINES."

APPENDIX 2

Excerpts from the Report of the Ad Hoc Committee on Equal Treatment and Opportunity at Camp Lejeune

(1) Many white officers and noncommissioned officers retain prejudices and deliberately practice them. The most manifestations lie in the racial stories, jokes, and references to and about blacks or black Marines. These continue to exist in both official and unofficial contacts. The result is obvious when made within the hearing of a black Marine. More insidious, perhaps, is the fact that the attitudes reflected are thus perpetrated among contemporaries and fostered in subordinates. Unfortunately, the major offenders in this regard are among the relatively senior officers and enlisted Marines.

(2) Some of the facilities of the local community remain segregated: housing, barber shops, bars, and amusement centers. Patronage of these facilities by officers and enlisted personnel of this command is, in fact, condonation of discrimination. In addition, failure to act on valid complaints of segregated facilities, as required by current directives, presently exists and continues to be a source of discouragement among black members of this command.

(b) A major and serious cause of racial tension results from the actions of military police in the Camp Lejeune area. The black Marines in your command are the special target for discriminatory actions by the military police. The black Marine believes that any incident in which blacks are involved is automatically treated as a racial incident by the military police. They believe that they are brutalized, unfairly and illegally detained, and inhumanly treated.

(c) The black Marine is particularly concerned that only results, and never causes, are the subject of disciplinary actions on official investigations when black Marines are involved. Whether real or imagined, every such incident is a racial incident and is quickly known by every black Marine in your command. Any such incident, regardless of how trivial, could flare up into a full-fledged riot.

(d) In the opinion of the black Marine, he has no official channel available to him by and through which he can obtain redress for complaints of discrimination. In essence request mast is not accomplishing the purpose for which it was intended. There is a reluctance on the part of your troop leaders, both officers and enlisted, to admit that racial problems exist within a unit or organization. Thus complaints seldom progress beyond company level, if they go that far. In any case, the black Marine has no confidence in request mast procedures. He seldom sees any results.

(3) An exception to this broad indictment is in the office of the division inspector. However, only a small percentage of complaints are brought to this source.

(e) Because racial tensions exist within the 2d Marine Division, black and white Marines tend to polarize. Action and reaction increase the polarity of white to white and black to black. As and if this trend continues, the danger of major racial incident increases.

(f) The black Marine exhibits unusual affinity and sympathy for members of his race.

(g) The absence of black representation in official photographs and drawings, such as career-planning posters and barbershop (acceptable-haircut) pictures, exemplify the subtle prejudice-by-omission and spread an undesirable effect in your command.

Generally speaking, the young Marines, black and white, who live and work closely together and who are both the subject and target of the problem, are striving for mutual accommodation. Their attempts are blocked and frustrated by the officers and noncommissioned officers, who, knowingly or unknowingly, intentionally or otherwise, prevent the full realization of your desired objectives. . . .

APPENDIX 3

Platoon Leader's Pamphlet on Racial Policies at Camp Lejeune

ITEMS FOR ACTION

1. *Policy.* It is the Commanding General's policy that every Marine in this Division shall receive equal treatment and be afforded equal opportunity. It is mandatory that the actions and attitudes of every officer and enlisted man conform to and exemplify this policy. All personnel will be assigned duty and responsibility, allowed privilege and benefit, and afforded equal justice regardless of race, creed, color, or nationality.

Within the bounds of law, order, military discipline, and the rights of others, all military personnel and their families are encouraged to assert their moral and legal rights; are encouraged to express themselves without fear of ridicule or threat of reprisal when those rights are abused; and are encouraged to expect a hearing and redress of such abuse. The immediate and continuing support of all the officers and men of the 2d Marine Division is mandatory.

Platoon leaders will assure that members of their platoons are informed of and comply with this policy.

2. *Procedure.* It is expected that platoon leaders will listen to and act upon complaints of alleged prejudice or discrimination. Judgment is required to separate those cases which are valid or imagined from those which may be mischievous. A complaint of the black Marine has been that even when complaints are heard, they are ignored. This may be interpreted correctly, or otherwise, as an assumption that the platoon leader is himself prejudiced. The assumption may be incorrect, but unless

228

the Marine is informed of action taken on his complaint, he has no cause to feel otherwise.

It is further required that the platoon leader conduct discussions with his assembled platoon on topics relating to 2d Marine Division policy and the related racial situation. Such a discussion must avoid stereotype (the "canned" lecture), and be free of dogmatic statements or implications such as those that indicate that simple answers will solve a serious and complicated situation. It is expected that individual Marines, if encouraged to participate, can provide and gain a deeper insight into the situation and those factors which tend to influence it.

3. *Statistics.* The following statistics are provided on black Marines in the Marine Corps and in the 2d Marine Division. It is significant to note the representation in the officer ranks. This is not a good situation and the Marine Corps is attempting to rectify it. The Marine Corps is seeking black officers in greater numbers than there are applicants. Current officer procurement programs will more than double the total number of black officers. However, the Marine Corps does experience a problem of retention of these individuals. The same proven or potential leadership qualities that benefit the Marine Corps are also in great demand in the civilian community, where perhaps the rewards are greater. The black career Marine is just on the threshold of advancement in the senior non-commissioned officer ranks where time-in-service and time-in-grade requirements as well as experience and ability must be considered. The opportunity for the black career Marine has never been greater than it is today. . . .

ITEMS FOR DISCUSSION

1. *Background.* The background of our black Marines before they entered the Marine Corps will explain, to some degree, how and why they react when confronted with a racial situation. Many have not had the advantages and privileges of most white Marines. They suffered low wages, menial jobs, poor housing, harassment, and exploitation. The black community has tended to bond together for mutual security, and the young black Marine is extremely sensitive to any event that affects his

race. Although the average Marine who is black does not complain about his past, and perhaps entered the Marine Corps to rise above it, incidents of real or imagined prejudice or discrimination bring forth latent resentment. To some extent and to varying degrees, he encounters his past in the environs of Camp Lejeune and when he goes home on leave or liberty. The young black Marine who does not harbor some resentment against the white community is the exception rather than the rule.

Consider the background of the white Marine. He enjoys the advantage his white skin has given him. To a remarkable extent he is not aware of either the conditions under which the black existed or his aspirations. While he agrees in principle with the policy of equality of treatment and opportunity, he may not understand just what that means. To some extent and to varying degrees the white Marine is advantaged by the situation he encounters in the environs of Camp Lejeune. He accepts the South as he finds it, sometimes without considering whether his black counterpart is also accepted.

It is against this background that we must find a solution to the racial situation that exists.

2. *Understanding.* The basis for a good racial relationship is an understanding of our actions and attitudes. The only real change can come about when we understand that the present unfavorable aspects of the racial situation stem from irrational human reaction. Change must come from within. While we cannot always expect to change an attitude, we can require a change in actions and hope that a change in attitude will follow. The effort to understand involves all races. This is so because Marines have always supported each other in all things and at all times—and must continue to do so. Therefore, each of us must thoroughly comprehend the matter, discuss it, clear the air of rumor, and see to it that we are in fact thoroughly mutually supporting.

The Marine who is black is extremely sensitive to real or imagined indications of racial prejudice or discrimination. He has developed modes of behavior, speech, dress, entertainment, and appearance which appeal to him and satisfy needs which he has. Neither his clothes, his haircut, his language, his dark glasses, his dancing habits, the music he listens to, the fact that he may wear a mustache, nor the fact that he enjoys the company of other Marines of his race are significant other than that they are as he prefers it. They are symbols of his race and he may be at a loss to explain why, any more than any other race can account for some of its actions or habits.

All Marines must be willing to accept and understand the black Marine on the basis of equality of treatment and opportunity. This may mean a change of previously held ideas and notions. The large majority of white Marines are trying. Many racial slurs and irritants are completely unintentional and occur because the white Marine does not understand what he has done.

On the other hand, the young white Marine must be accorded his due. He is willing to accept the Marine who is black on the basis of equality of treatment and opportunity, but he cannot be expected to respond favorably to unreasonable demand or provocation which transgresses upon his own rights.

Finally, recognize that our Marines will encounter racial extremists of both races. It is the action and the instigation of this small percentage of die-hards that may cause minor racial incidents to flare into racial problems. These are the individuals who cause the trouble— trouble that someone else always pays for.

It is against this background of understanding that specific irritants, as they relate to the racial situation, are discussed.

3. *Irritants*

a. On the rare occasion when it is necessary to refer to the Marine who is black as such, the only acceptable term is just that, "black Marine." Any other terms such as "boy," "spook," "splib," "negro," "Uncle Tom," "nigra," "nigger," or "colored" carry connotations of prejudice and must be avoided. The white Marine equally resents "cracker," "honkie," "white pig," "whitey," and "redneck," and the use of such terms will foster an unfavorable reaction.

b. Black Marines, as do white Marines, have a tendency

to gather in racial groups. The black Marine on observing such a group may resent his exclusion. The white Marine may feel that such a group of black Marines is plotting trouble. Black Marines, in particular, resent the suspicion that is usually directed their way. Marines of both races should make a particular effort to integrate groups whenever feasible. If this is done, all suspicions and aspersions are automatically voided. The policy of granting liberty by fire team by deployed units is a good example of group integration.

c. Uniform regulations of the Marine Corps and the Navy authorize the wearing of *neatly kept* mustaches. Arbitrary standards and contrary policies established by the lower echelons of command affect the black Marine more than the white in that he feels that they are directed against his race.

d. For the black Marine, the "Afro" haircut style is "in." Such a haircut is not necessarily contrary to Marine Corps standards of appearance. Pictures of such acceptable haircuts are on display in all Marine Corps exchange barber shops. The young black Marine deeply resents arbitrary standards established by a white officer or NCO which forces him to adopt a more "customary" hair style.

e. Allegations of duty and billet assignment based upon race are prevalent. The black Marine is sensitive to indications that menial tasks are given mostly to him, or a duty or billet assignment is based upon race. Of equal significance is the effect of such assignment on the black Marine, who observes the black Marine in such assignments and jumps to wrong conclusions. Particular care must be taken to assure that race is not a factor in assignments of any type.

f. Allegations that the granting or denial of privilege based upon race are also heard. As an example, the black Marine may conclude that 96-hour passes are granted to more white Marines than to black Marines. Again, the effect of such granting or denial on the black Marine who observes and jumps to wrong conclusions must be considered.

g. The use of signs, symbols, and gestures which inflame or incite a race is a frequent source of irritation. It is perhaps the circumstances under which they are used and a misunderstanding as to intent that is the source. The display of the "Dixie" flag is particularly irritating to the black Marine because of slavery aspects of the Civil War and its more recent use in anti-civil rights demonstrations. The flag is, on the other hand, deeply cherished by many white Marines as a symbol of the courage and sacrifice of Americans for a cause and because it is a part of some state flags. "Black Power" symbol and gestures are resented by some white Marines, who associate them with militant dissention. To the typical black Marine, such symbols and gestures represent a unity, an esprit, and a lawful aspiration. The use of any signs, symbols, or gestures for the purpose of inciting or antagonizing or when they convey disrespect for authority is prohibited and is cause for disciplinary action.

h. The use of black officers and NCO's out of the chain of command to dispose of "problems" involving black Marines is resented by all black Marines and jeopardizes those officers and NCO's and the respect accorded them. The black Marine interprets this as a fear or a reluctance on the part of his white platoon leader or the NCO's over him to get involved.

i. Some platoon leaders and NCO's do discuss the racial situation with their troops. But sometimes they segregate them into black and white groups to do it. This practice is resented by all troops and is obvious segregation.

j. Some platoon leaders and NCO's do not discuss the racial situation with their troops. This is interpreted variously as a reluctance, an unwillingness to prevent discriminatory practices, or an indication of personal prejudice. Obviously, compliance with the requirements of this pamphlet will remedy this situation.

k. The thoughts and feelings of the white Marine must be considered and discussed. The white NCO who is accused of prejudice by a black Marine who doesn't like a task he was assigned, the lines at the mess hall or the movie which are rudely cut into by a group of black Marines, the catcalls and jeers when a white is killed on a movie screen, excessively loud "soul" music in the barracks—these and similar intentional acts that flout discipline and courtesy do nothing but worsen the situation, do not benefit anyone, and will not be ignored.

4. *Summary*. The platoon leader must express a positive attitude concerning the racial situation in the 2d Marine Division. He must be willing to discusss all aspects of the issues and seek to creat understanding among his troops. The challenge is presented. Fundamentally, it is no different from others faced as a leader. To avoid it or neglect it is to fail. Meet the challenge with mental awareness and tenacity. Your success will make you "stand tall" among your fellow Marines!

APPENDIX 4

Commandant's Directive on Racial Relations and Instances of Racial Violence within the Marine Corps

1. During the past several months there have been instances among Marines of violence and other unacceptable actions which apparently stem from racial differences. Such problems are almost unheard of among Marines in combat. It is when Marines move to other areas or return to the United States that these differences arise. And it is there where acts of violence beween Marines are occurring, acts which cannot be tolerated and must stop.

2. I do not believe that the recent events are typical. In fact, literally thousands of Marines have quietly made the adjustment from combat, and capably served stern and demanding tours of duty, in a national atmosphere where expressions of appreciation for their services are hard to find. It is evident, however, that despite our substantial progress toward racial parity, difficulties of a significant nature do exist in our corps.

3. It is now and has long been our policy in the Marine Corps that discrimination in any form is not tolerated. It has similarly been our policy that a fighting organization such as ours must have a solid foundation of firm, impartial discipline. It is in the context of these two basic policies that we must take measures to dispel the racial problems that currently exist.

4. We may argue that the underlying causes of our racial difficulties parallel those of the nation at large, but the fact remains that they are real, and they can

adversely affect the military effectiveness of our Corps. We must seek in every manner possible to improve understanding among all Marines, stressing the concept that we are a band of comrades in arms, a loyal fraternity with a traditional esprit that spans an era of nearly two hundred years. The truly integrated spirit that pervades on the battlefield must pervade in the barracks and on liberty as well. The causes of friction, rather than the symptoms, must be identified by all commanders, frankly and openly discussed, and eliminated where possible. Positive and overt efforts to eradicate every trace of discrimination, whether intentional or not, must be continued. Actions or influences that tend to arouse antagonism between fellow Marines must be combated. Every Marine must understand that the Marine Corps does guarantee equal rights, equal opportunity, and equal protection without regard to race and will continue to do so. We take care of our own, continuing to recognize, as the foundation of our Corps, the importance, integrity, and dignity of the individual Marine.

5. Equally vital, each Marine must understand why the Marine Corps has always demanded the highest standards in military appearance, military courtesy, and proficiency, and why we will continue to do so. These high standards breed pride, and pride, in turn, builds the kind of discipline that is essential to battlefield success with minimum casualties. These qualities have always been the hallmark of Marines and no relaxation in our proven high standards will be condoned. For example, uniforms will be worn correctly with no non-regulation items in evidence; haircuts will conform to regulations, no more, no less; proper military salutes will be rendered on appropriate occasions; the highest quality of professionalism must be exhibited in every assignment; breaches of good order and discipline will be dealt with fairly, expeditiously, and firmly. This is especially true for those Marines who instigate or execute violence against their fellow Marines.

6. It is the responsibility of the officers and staff NCO's to provide the leadership and set the example for those junior to them, particularly for the combat veterans who

have had little experience in other duties. We must demonstrate that leadership responsibilities demand after-hours availability and supervision. I cannot improve upon the expression of principles of leadership and the relations between officers, staff NCO's, and men as they are written in the Marine Corps Manual. If these were conscientiously carried out, many of our problems would disappear.

7. Some complaints about discrimination I have heard appear to be valid, but many are based on rumor or misapprehension. Nevertheless, some Marines believe them to be true. Most are concerned with promotions, military justice, duty assignments, and request mast. It is essential that all comrades learn of these erroneous beliefs and systemically and continuously inform their men of the facts. Commanders and staff NCO's must communicate with their men and see that they get the straight word so that trust in the Corps can be restored in those who doubt.

8. To come to grips with the problem of racial friction, the following actions will be immediately undertaken:

a. The contents of this ALMAR will at once be read and explained to all Marines, except to those in combat, by immediate commanding officers personally.

b. All officers and NCO's will review the complete contents of the Department of the Navy's Manual on equal opportunity and treatment of military personnel.

c. All officers and staff NCO's will read, carefully absorb, and practice the contents of that section of the Marine Corps Manual dealing with military leadership.

d. Every commanding officer will review his request mast procedures to ensure that all Marines understand clearly their right to air their grievances witout hindrance or prejudice. I emphasize that no harassment, either real or implied, will be permitted to occur at any level between the individual requesting mast and the commander with whom he is requesting mast. Individuals may request mast with any commanding officer/commanding general in their chain of command at their base or location. I want to insure that channels of communications between every Marine and his commanding officer are open, that every Marine understands that they are open, and that legitimate grievances will receive sympathetic consideration and rapid response.

e. Commanders will permit the Afro/natural haircut providing it conforms with current Marine Corps regulations.

f. No actions, signs, symbols, gestures, and words that are contrary to tradition will be permitted during formations or when rendering military courtesies to colors, the national anthem, or individuals. Individual signs between groups or individuals will be accepted for what they are— gestures or recognition and unity; in this connection, it is Marine Corps policy that, while such actions are to be discouraged, they are nevertheless expressions of individual belief and are not, in themselves, prohibited. However, they are grounds for disciplinary actions if executed during official ceremonies or in a manner suggesting direct defiance of duly constituted authority.

g. Each commander will review his promotion procedures to verify their fairness and emphasis on merit and potential, and will correct any errors that may have been made in the past, in accordance with current regulations.

h. Commanding generals and commanding officers will immediately, conscientiously, and persistently execute the general and specific provisions of this ALMAR and report progress to me from time to time through the chain of command. . . .

Index

239